Unlikely Reward

by

Vicky Kaseorg

1

The boat slammed into shore and sent the driver headlong into the windshield, which resulted in a lot of blood and gore, not to mention questions. However, maybe I better fill you in on some background before I tell you what happened next.

Mom asked if she could go shopping for a wedding dress with me. I told her she could go without me. Pick one out. The last thing I wanted to do was shop for a wedding dress, let alone wear it. I mean I was good with marrying Hank, but the whole dress up like a princess didn't fit my mojo.

Besides, it was Family Dollar or Better-Mart for the bewitching bridal gown. If there was another clothes store in Kumsquat, I was unfamiliar with it. Sometimes the Kumsquat gas station sold t-shirts, but I had not yet seen a wedding gown there.

On top of my aversion to anything other than my (usually) swamp-encrusted jeans, I had an ailing hawk to take care of. I was the new (only) employee of the Kumsquat Raptor Center, which incidentally was also founded by me since I happened to chance upon two eagles that needed emergency housing. That is another long story. We can skim over all but the most critical facts. One eagle I caught in my bare hands when he fell out of a tree, and the other I chanced upon just as she was shot out of the sky. Unlikely, yes, but so is the delicate balance of life on Earth yet here we are.

The only other really pertinent info you need to know about me is I just became a Christian about two minutes before Hank asked me to marry him. I am brand new to this Holy Guacamole stuff, so be sure to cut me some slack if you see some questionable behavior. It takes time to do a makeover on the runaway teen progeny of a drug addict and a drunk.

"You want me to buy your wedding dress without you?" Mom asked.

Oh. You may be wondering how I went from 'runaway teen of drunk mother' to asking that same mother to buy my wedding dress without me. That's another long story. She stopped drinking, found Jesus, and worked pretty hard to show me she was a changed woman. And about my dad. He died of a drug overdose. Humanity shed no tears over that loss, believe me. (Probably not a Christian thing to say, but remember that bit about cutting me slack.)

"I'm not picky," I assured Mom.

Like, *no-duh!* All you had to do was take a gander at my current get-up to figure that out. I had three sets of clothes in my wardrobe. My work clothes for when I used to work at Better-Mart, my shorts and 99 cent t-shirt from the grocery store that said "Buy-Low, save big", and then my jeans and another t-shirt. That cold weather outfit was completed by a red hoodie.

"I'm not sure you should not at least approve what I find," Mom said.

"Oh, I approve."

"I haven't bought it yet," she reminded me. "And you probably will need to try it on."

In case you are wondering, my mom was no fashionista herself, and she wasn't certain I would need to try it on. She used the word 'probably' honestly. She didn't know if wedding dresses somehow miraculously conformed to the bride's size, being as she had never had a wedding dress.

"We're about the same size," I said, glancing at her and making a wild guess, "You try it on and send me a text photo."

"Well then, that is exciting," she said, squeezing her hands together.

Good. One less thing to worry about. I would have been fine eloping and skipping all the hoopla, but Hank and his parents were the doting sort and wanted a real wedding, with a real pastor, and (as they said it) "sanctified vows before God." That kind of scared me because it sounded so serious. Don't get me wrong. I know marriage is forever but sealing the deal with God was new to me on all fronts.

I had put my foot down on one wedding detail. My dolphin friends, horse, dog, and eagles had to be invited. That meant it had to take place on my property along the Suwannee. No church could accommodate an interspecies affair with land, sea, and air creatures.

Hank agreed to that instantly. Mom said she would plant flowers which raised a few eyebrows. As far as I knew, Mom had never, not once, owned a plant or touched a seed. However, I was not going to rain on that parade since she was trying so hard to overcome her lifetime of neglecting me due to her alcohol abuse.

Hank's mom wanted to help as well, but she was limited on the account of having a fatal disease. However, I assured her that whatever she wanted to do, just do it. No need to ask. I wouldn't know if it was a good idea or not since this was my first wedding.

I mean, not only had I never been married (remember I was only nineteen) but I had also never even been to a wedding. I may have seen one on TV once but that was about the full extent of my exposure. I knew the basics that were required: a bride and groom, someone to read a bunch of googly-eyed vows, and cake.

"Well," Hank said when I asked if that was all we needed, "There is usually an exchange of rings."

I frowned. "Where do we get those?"

"We pick them out together at a jewelry store."

"Does Kumsquat have a jewelry store?"

"No, we may have to travel to Orlando for that. We could make a day of it."

Already this wedding business was getting complicated. Harry the Hawk was still recuperating from a very bad injury. His leg and his wing were broken. I could not leave him the entire day.

Hank, as usual, knew just what I was thinking. That is part of why I agreed to this aggravation of a wedding. Hank was about the most considerate person on earth and if he wanted a proper wedding, I suppose, being the bride, I should oblige.

"Leah, I know you are worried about Harry, but Dad has already agreed to come look in on him several times a day, and your mom even offered to help."

Mom? She was very squeamish and knew nothing about hawk rehabilitation. Neither did I really, but with a few months under my belt of working with the two eagles I rescued, I had an inkling. Besides, Dr. Pritchett, the avian vet, and Mr. Forrest (Hank's dad and a certified eagle rehabilitator) were both supervising me.

"I don't think cutting up mouse chunks and helping the hawk poop are up Mom's alley."

"I think you might be surprised. She sounded genuinely eager. The advantage of training her is you would have an assistant."

"I don't really need an assistant to care for one hawk."

"No, but any day another injured bird could be brought in."

He was right about that. The two eagles I had successfully returned to the wild had been found within a few days of each other. OK, maybe you need to know just a little about that story. Or you could just read the book I wrote about it. I was a "promising" young author according to my publisher, and they were very excited as I kept churning out sequels loosely based on my life.

But in case you are a cheapskate and don't want to buy my books, here is the summary of how I ended up leaving my promising career as a *Senior Dressing Room Manager* at Better-Mart and became the one employee of the Kumsquat Raptor Center.

Like I said earlier, I caught the baby eagle when he was shoved out of his nest by a murderous sibling. I was not legally allowed to try to raise him, but the nearest Eagle Rehab center was too far away and overfull with injured eagles. Lo and behold, they wanted to build a satellite center in my neck of the woods. They already knew about Dr. Pritchett who resided in my area and was a well-known avian vet. They didn't know Hank's dad was licensed to work with injured eagles. He is a U.S. Fish and Wildlife Service officer, and had worked with injured raptors off and on, enough to be licensed. As long as he supervised me, I could be trained to work with the eagle, and the Florida Raptor Center was willing to build a small facility. (They called it a hacking tower, but I called it an aviary because hacking sounds illegal.)

Then, as luck would have it, though Hank would say there is no such thing as luck, an eagle was shot by a poacher and landed practically at my feet just a few days later. That injured eagle was added to our aviary residents, and it turned out to be the eaglet's mother. I called the eaglet Tippy and the mother Baldy.

Anyway, the Florida Raptor Center built our aviary in record time, and with Mr. Forrest's supervision, I helped both the eagles recuperate and be ready for release. Tippy was probably not going to hang around our tree nest a whole lot longer. He was becoming better and better at hunting, and was gone for many hours sometimes. Baldy split time between our nest and her other eaglet's nest. She supplemented food for them both with the help of her mate who stayed mostly at the other nest.

It's possible both eagles would be gone by the time the wedding rolled around. Hank and I had not set a date yet, but he said it would take some time to plan.

So, the Florida Raptor Center offered to employ me since no one else wanted to live in Kumsquat to run the new aviary. They didn't tell me that. They said they would employ me because I had done such a good job with the eagles, but I didn't do much. Mostly I caught fish to feed them. However, I didn't argue. I was happy to retire from Better-Mart. With the little salary the Raptor Center offered and my modest royalty checks from my books, I made enough money to survive.

I had taken one class at the Kumsquat Kommunity Kollege, but since I was doing what I wanted to be doing, decided when the semester ended that I would take a break from higher education. I did miss my composition teacher, Miss Mickleburr, but she promised to visit now and then.

So now you know anything worth knowing. Except the boat crash story. I'm getting to that. Learning to delay gratification is a sign of maturity so hang on to your horses!

Back to Hank and the discussion of wedding necessities.

"OK, so once we get the rings, are we all set?"

"Well, we need a pastor willing to come and officiate. Are you good with Pastor Rimerton if he will agree to it?"

Pastor Rimerton was the father of the little girl who had been abducted about a year ago. With the help of my animal friends, I found the little girl safe and sound. That's another unlikely story that just happens to be true. Again, read about it if you can afford the paltry price of my book. If not, you are missing out on a great story.

"I would love Pastor Rimerton to marry us!" I said.

Pastor Rimerton was also the pastor of the church Mom attended. I had been to church with her many times, but only once or twice since becoming a Christian. Even back in the days when I thought his God was about as believable as the Easter Bunny, Pastor Rimerton was kind to me. Hank and I had started attending Pastor Rimerton's church, but life had interfered several times… like in the form of murderous poachers, child abductors, and reeling, recovering raptors.

"And then," Hank continued, "We probably ought to think about a honeymoon."

This stopped me in my tracks. I couldn't think of a single place I'd rather be than with my animals on the banks of the Suwannee in the cute little fishing hut that Hank and I would rent, with the distant option to own. I had lusted after that fishing hut more fervently than I lusted after Hank (is it ok for a new Christian to speak this way???). In fact, I was dying to get married ASAP so I could move into that hut.

As always, Hank knew just what I was thinking, and that I was worried about my furry, finned, and flying friends. "My dad and your mom have already promised to take care of the animals. I thought we could go somewhere you have always wanted to go for a few days."

I thought about that. Had I ever wanted to go somewhere other than away from my drugged and drunken parents? I had never really wanted to go TO someplace…only AWAY from my childhood home.

"I wouldn't know where that might be," I admitted.

"We don't have to go on a honeymoon," Hank said.

I detected some disappointment. While I had only been in my blissful home on the Suwannee for two years, Hank had been here his whole life. He probably didn't look at it with the same sense of blissful wonder that I did.

"Why don't you pick a place?" I asked.

He smiled at me and wrapped me in his arms. "We can think about it. I'll talk with Pastor Rimerton today and we can set a date. We need to work out a guest list."

Again, this stymied me. The only person outside of Hank that I really cared to be there was my mom. I had to think hard who else I might want to invite, or who else might even want to come.

"For example," Hank said, detecting my problem, "Miss Mickleburr and Miss Beam think of you as their friend."

They did? I guess they did. Miss Mickleburr once told me I was the most gifted student she had ever taught. Of course, my composition class was the first class she had ever taught, but her praise still warmed me. Miss Beam was my manager at my first job in Kumsquat at the Better-Mart. I had seen some sparks flying between her and the policeman who helped me solve the Rimerton abduction case. Officer William Spear had asked me out, but then Hank asked me to marry him and William moved on. Nonetheless, he was a friend, and since he didn't carry a torch for me anymore, maybe I should ask him as well.

"It's okay to just have a few people," Hank said.

At the time of this conversation, we were sitting on the bank of the Suwannee. It was a mild sunny day like it was about 364 out of 365 days of the year in Florida. The sky was freckled with some clouds, and there was a wisp of a breeze carrying the scent of rotting swamp creatures. Hank was fishing. We often cut up the fish he caught and fed the little chunks to Harry the Hawk.

Harry had only been with us for a few weeks, and was recuperating. You don't want to hear about all I had to do in the first week or so of his convalescence. It involved helping him poop which he couldn't do on his own since he couldn't stand upright after breaking his wing and leg. Now he could, and could also perch independently. It would still be a few weeks before he'd be able to fly, but he was beginning to stretch his wing. Dr. Pritchett, the avian vet came twice a week to show me how to exercise Harry's wing to keep it limber for flight. He came to change the dressing and assess the wound which was healing nicely. Mostly I watched, but sometimes Dr. Pritchett would supervise and let me actually help mobilize Harry's wing.

I still hadn't been allowed to capture and contain Harry since that took more experience and practice than I had at this point in my rehab career. Mr. Forrest (Hank's dad) was the Fish and Wildlife Services Agent who was officially training me and he or Dr. Pritchett were always the ones to do that so far. Mr. Forrest told me that when they got in a smaller bird that I wasn't likely to kill or be killed by, they would give me a chance to hone my bird-tackling technique. That's not what they called it but that is sort of what it looked like.

Anyway, I was the one responsible for feeding Harry, and for cleaning his cage. Hank loved to fish, and so he was a great help catching Harry's dinner. I used to have to feed my eagles while they were recuperating, but now Baldy was completely healed and she made sure her fledgling Tippy had food when he returned from the hunt empty-taloned. Which was often.

Hank hadn't had much luck so far reeling in some dinner for Harry when there was a big commotion in the middle of the river. A bunch of fish were leaping into the air like popcorn popping. Flash, the first dolphin who had greeted and befriended me when I was a hopeless runaway just arriving in Kumsquat, now arched his back out of the water. I knew it was him because I could identify the notch on his dorsal fin, which was different from the fin that surfaced beside him. That was Pinky, his daughter. They were the two friendliest ones of the pod of four regulars that showed up along my shoreline.

It was obvious they had come to help. They herded the leaping fish in our direction and then disappeared. Within minutes, Hank hauled in a nice sized largemouth bass.

"Thanks!" he called out, though the dolphins were gone.

You see why I didn't need a honeymoon. What could top a place like this with friends like these?

My mother slammed the door of our single-wide, and marched over to us.

"I'm off to find you a wedding dress!" she said.

Hank looked puzzled. I hadn't told him yet that my mom would be the one picking out my wedding dress. Honestly, you would think after two years of knowing me that nothing would surprise him, but this did.

"Oh. It's ok, Leah. I can chop this up for Harry and feed him if you need to get going now."

"No. It's fine. Mom knows what to look for."

Hank tilted his head, eyebrows scrunched. He didn't comment.

Mom filled the silence. "White. Fancy. Size 2. Anything else I need to know?"

I glanced at my feet. We all did, envisioning my muddy flip-flops with the fancy, white wedding dress.

"Size 7 shoes?" she asked.

I nodded. Hank tossed her a weak smile.

"I bet I can find all of those in Kernersville," Mom said. Kernersville was the next town over and about double the size of Kumsquat. Its Main Street was a full mile long. I could not recall a single clothes store there, other than Goodwill, but I'd only been there once. She tucked her purse under her arm and headed off to the rust-bucket that masqueraded as her car.

"Good luck," Hank called, his voice a little dubious. Maybe he was also picturing the little Goodwill store and visualizing the get-up in which his bride would be walking down the aisle. Remember, the aisle would be a swamp mud path leading from the horse pasture to the reedy mucky shore. I wondered if he was considering calling the whole thing off, but he shrugged and returned to dicing up the bass.

Then, as though Hank were not making one of the absolute most stupendous pronouncements of all time, he didn't even look up and said, "You can move into the fishing hut tomorrow. That gives you some space to be alone before our wedding."

"Tomorrow? The hut will be my home tomorrow?"

"Yep. If you want it. Then it will be our home after the wedding, whenever that will be."

"Oh Hank!" I cried, throwing my arms around his neck and almost piercing myself with the fish hook. "How did you manage that??"

"The owner was happy to have us rent a little early, and I thought you might like it."

I was ready to gush with even more joy when suddenly, the little motorboat came careening around the hairpin turn in the river just south of my shore and roared straight towards us. Both Hank and I scrambled to our feet, but would have been smashed flat like flounders if the driver hadn't wrenched the steering bar at the last moment and slammed into the muddy bank twenty feet from us.

An explosive smack startled the eagles who took flight, and Lightning snorted, her neck snapping upright from her (fruitless) grazing. Zippy erupted in a series of high pitched howls, and dashed off to the crash site. Hank dropped the fish and we both zipped after Zippy.

A woman was slumped across the boat steering wheel. The motor idled briefly and then coughed to a sputtering stop. Her long blond hair fell across her unconscious face, but it was still obvious that she was beautiful, even with a face quickly purpling with bruises from the impact.

The clothes she wore were scant, and tight. The tiny spandex skirt barely covered her bottom. I couldn't imagine why she would be in such an outfit to drive a motorboat. This was not your typical fishing costume. The stilettos on her feet were the same bright red as her toenails and the drops of blood dripping from her head onto her big toe.

"Ma'am!" Hank said, "Are you okay?"

This is what I would call a rhetorical question. The vampy blond agreed I think, since she didn't answer. She was breathing so I knew she was alive, but I didn't know for how much longer.

Then she groaned, and slowly lifted her head. Blood dripped from a gash on her forehead into her eyes.

"Where am I?" she asked.

"Kumsquat," Hank said, "You crashed your boat. Are you alright?"

She pressed her hand to her wound and sucked in a breath. "I think I'm bleeding."

I didn't say *Thank you Captain Obvious*, probably because I was now a Christian.

"Here." Hank reached in his pocket and pulled out a wad of tissues. "Hold this against that cut."

She did so, pushing a few bloody blond strands of hair behind her ear.

"We can call an ambulance…" he said.

"No!" She shouted with what appeared to be a mixture of fear and guilt. She added more quietly, "I'm fine. Just shook up."

She stood up slowly, while I watched to see if the micro-skirt would maintain the meager chance it had of keeping her underwear under wraps. It did. Barely.

"I just got the boat…" she said. "I guess I haven't quite got the hang of driving it yet."

Ya think??? Again, I kept that observation to myself. Thanks be to God.

She looked around, holding the tissue against her forehead. Mom now appeared by our side. She had been pulling out when the boat slammed into our shore. I guess the noise had made her turn back.

"You sure must have been in a hurry," Mom said.

The woman's eyes teared up, and she blinked to keep them from spilling over.

"I was running away. I guess I was going too fast for that turn."

"What were you running from?" Mom asked.

"A man determined to kill me!" she said angrily.

All our eyes popped open at this revelation.

"Is he chasing you in a boat?" Hank asked.

"No…not that I know of. I don't think he knows I'm gone yet. But I decided today was the day I would leave. I had to. My life has been one long torment after another."

Mom's face softened. I knew she could relate. Honestly, so could I.

"Where were you headed?" Mom asked.

"Away," she said. "No place special. Just anyplace where he wasn't."

She pulled the wad of bloody tissue from the cut in her head. The blood had slowed down considerably. It was not nearly as bad a cut as it had first appeared. She was lucky.

"Is that your trailer?" she asked, pointing.

We all glanced at my single wide. I nodded.

She pursed her mouth, as though she desperately wanted to say something but didn't dare. Mom understood her hesitancy instantly. I assume Mom had been in a similar mess many times in her brutal upbringing.

"Do you need a safe place to stay?" Mom asked gently.

The woman's tears sparkled in her eyes again and she nodded.

Maybe it was the new Holy Spirit in me, or maybe just a moment of craziness, but I put my hand on her arm. "We have an open bed. You are in luck. I am moving out this afternoon."

2

I know. It was an irrational, impulsive offer. And selfish. I wanted to move into the hut ASAP. Mom hadn't yet heard about the hut, so she glared at me. She was sure I was booting her from the trailer in favor of the blond lady with her teeny tiny skirt.

I brought her up to speed about the hut while Hank helped the woman step out of the boat. That was when we noticed water in the bottom of the boat and the gash in the hull from the accident. The woman's thin spiky heels sank four inches into the muck as she stepped onto our shore.

"I'm not really dressed for the swamp," she admitted.

I wanted so badly to ask her exactly what she was dressed for, but decided it best to keep those ponderings to myself. Let's just say I had my suspicions.

She removed the shoes, and her neat red toenails sank into the muck. She smiled, looking down.

"This reminds me of when I was a kid playing in the mud."

Flash, my dolphin buddy, took that moment to shove his nose out of the water and emit a staccato series of clicks and squeaks. The lady shrieked and swung around. All she saw was his fin as he submerged.

"Shark!"

"It's not a shark," I said, "That's a dolphin. His name is Flash."

"How do you know his name?" she asked.

I blinked at her.

Pinky then rose out of the water, even closer to us than Flash, and smacked her tail on the surface of the river. It sent a spray of water across all of us, but really doused the woman.

"That's Pinky," I said.

"Are they tame?" she asked, running as quickly as the muck would allow.

"Usually," I said.

She hurried out of the shallow water, though both dolphins had said their piece and now disappeared.

"Did you steal the boat?" Mom asked. I could always count on her to say what was on her mind.

"No," the woman said. "A friend gave it to me."

This sounded fishy. I studied the woman's face as she turned to my mother. She was older than she had first appeared. She had used makeup to full advantage, and from a distance she would have passed for twenty. Up close, I realized she was closer to my mom's age. She was definitely past the age when she should be wearing skirts that just grazed the edges of arrest.

"I only need a place to stay for a little while. I don't think he'll look for me very long. I have money. I can pay my way."

"If someone is after you, why don't you call the police?" I asked.

"They won't do a thing," she said with a snort. "They will go after him after I'm dead. Not before." She said this with disgust, and I believed her.

"Come with me," Mom said, "We can get you cleaned up and I have some clothes you can wear."

I wondered if she would protest since Mom's clothes offered at least 75% more coverage than hers. However, she nodded, and followed Mom passively towards the trailer. Hank raised his eyebrows, watching them and probably, like me, wondering how long that tiny skirt would win the battle against revealing her buttocks.

"I wonder if she is an accountant," I said when they were out of earshot.

Hank chuckled, but didn't comment on my snarkiness.

"I hope Mom doesn't bring her along for my wedding dress shopping."

At this, Hank shook his head. "Leah."

"I know. Sorry."

That was the only rebuke he would offer. He quickly changed the subject. "I can help you pack your things for the hut. My mom has been busy. She bought a few things and has been getting it ready for us. I hope you will like it."

"Oh Hank. I have wanted that hut forever! I would like it if I had to sleep on the bare floor!"

"Would you like to see it now?" he asked. "I think your mom can get her settled. Maybe find out what the story really is." Mom and the blond had disappeared into the trailer.

"As soon as I feed Harry!"

Harry the hawk was perched in his small cage. It had been a little while since he could perch without toppling. I was pleased with his progress.

Hank had recently completed our tiny "medical exam room" adjoining our aviary. It had a mini-fridge where I kept the raptor food sent from a facility upstate. For the eagles, we had provided fish out of my river that we caught ourselves. The hawk ate mostly rodents and I drew the line at catching and dissecting rodents into bitesize chunks.

There was an examination table, and even a portable x-ray machine. That was brand new, bought with money from the poacher's fine. My animals and I had been instrumental in catching the poacher that tried to kill Baldy, and the huge fine he and his partner were slapped with helped pay my salary and build our medical room.

So far, I hadn't used the x-ray machine, but Dr. Pritchett, the avian vet who supervised me along with Hank's dad told me I could help when the next injured raptor came in and he would teach me how to use it.

For now, I grabbed a little baggie of rodent delight, and dumped it in a small steel bowl for Harry. I put the bowl of cut up rodents in his cage on the floor of a shelf near the perch. He waited till I had closed the little feed door and then hopped onto the shelf and ripped into the rodent pieces.

The eagles who were in the open aviary had taken flight when the boat crashed and had not returned. They were gone for longer and longer periods each day. Like any mother, I grieved that one day they would not return and my brief sojourn as an eagle parent would end.

Lightning nickered and came plodding over to the edge of the fence to get a rubdown. I scratched her behind her ears and she shivered with delight as I moved down her neck. She nuzzled my tummy. Zippy glanced our way from his sacked-out position in the sun, and then closed his eyes again. The excitement of the boat crash had worn off and he was ready to nap.

"She's lying," I said.

"Yes," Hank agreed, "But her fear is real."

That was probably true. I knew she wasn't on the up and up with the details of what she was running from, but she was running from something that scared her to death. I knew the signs well enough from personal experience.

Hank followed me towards the trailer so I could let Mom know we were heading to the hut.

"May as well grab my things too if Lolita will be spending the night with my mom," I said.

I realized as Hank scowled at my name for the scantily clad blond that I didn't know her name. Not one of us had asked. So, when we walked into the trailer, that was the first thing I rectified.

"I never got your name," I said, "I am Leah."

The blond was sitting on the couch with a cup of coffee in hand. Mom sat next to her, and both had obviously been engaged in some serious conversation. The blond's eyes were glistening from recent tears.

"Lolita," she said.

Hank coughed, but covered it up quickly by pounding on his chest. I was not so clever and could not prevent the eruption of giggles that boiled over.

"I'm sorry," I said, "Hank just told me the funniest thing on the way over."

Lolita didn't look like she believed my lame cover-up, and for sure Hank didn't. He coughed a few more times, while looking sideways at me.

Mom hopped into the awkward social moment. "Lolita was just telling me about her abusive work situation. Sexual harassment if ever I heard it!"

We nodded, at a bit of a loss for words probably for the same reason. Both of us were hard pressed not to notice that a mere millimeter separated Lolita's skirt from creeping up past the point of no return. I am not into blame the victim sort of mentality, but I have to say that if Lolita went to court to press charges, she might want to lower her hem a bit.

"I just wanted out," Lolita explained. "And then he threatened me. Said if I left or if I said anything, he would kill me."

I glanced out the window at the boat by the shore. It was clear it had filled with a few feet of water now and was listing to the right.

"Does your friend want his boat back?" I asked.

"Yikes!" Hank said, following my gaze. "Let's see if we can pull that up on shore."

He hurried off, first gathering wood planks that the boat could skid onto and support the keel off the ground. He was resourceful and strong. I figured the long rope I saw him attaching to the boat prow was to tie to his car so he could haul the boat in. It was a small motorboat, but still probably weighed more than he could drag to shore himself.

"We have a really great police friend," I assured her, "If you wanted to talk with him…"

"NO!" she cried again. "He meant what he said. I can't involve the police. He won't find me here. I just want to start a new life and forget he ever existed."

It was obvious there was more to this story. However, her fear and her tears were real. Whatever her past had been, she was honestly afraid.

"My things are in a small suitcase in the boat," she said. "I have some money. I can have the boat repaired and then will be on my way. I guess. Do you think it can be fixed?"

She looked at me as though I would have the slightest idea.

"Hank would know better."

Mom patted Lolita's knee. "You stay as long as you need. I know what it's like to run from your past."

Probably no truer words ever spoken than that.

"I'll gather my things and you can have the back bedroom," I said.

"You all are very kind," Lolita said, sniffling.

I scurried away, wondering what the truth was behind all that dripping mascara. My things all fit in one large backpack. Like I had told Hank, I knew what it was like to be on the run. I had few possessions, and even having been in my own safe place for two years now, traveled light. I guess I hadn't really lived down the fear that one day, I might have to run again.

Living in the coveted fishing hut might go a long ways towards helping me settle down. When I first met Hank, his father had not yet sold the hut. That blessed day, I saw Hank emerge from that magical little hut looking like a Greek God. He had been fishing off the deck of the hut which was perched on the end of a pier that extended over the water. The hut was perfect. Weathered grey siding with baby blue shutters. It looked so gentle and inviting, with the waves lapping at the piles, the wood posts that supported the pier and dock.

I gathered my few clothes, my laptop, and my bible and was ready to go. I finished packing before Hank had completed hauling the boat safely onto the wood blocks. He peered underneath examining the gash.

"Can it be fixed?" I asked.

"Probably," he said.

Hank can fix anything, another of his amazing attributes. When God was handing out talents, he double-dipped when He came to Hank.

"We'll cover it with a tarp," he said, "In case Lolita's boss comes snooping around."

"I don't think her name is really Lolita," I said. He chuckled, shaking his head.

"She's hiding something," I said. "Do you think my mom is safe?"

Even as I said that, I knew my mom could hold her own against pretty much anyone. She had not been trained on the streets for nothing. I'd once seen her fight off a gang of drugged men trying to break into my dad's meth lab. I'm not sure if she was protecting me, or the meth. Either way, she'd be fine with Lolita. Hank agreed.

Once the boat was hidden under the tarp, Hank took my backpack from me and we decided to walk rather than drive to the hut. It was only a quarter mile. Maybe it was only a short distance physically, but it was a huge leap for me emotionally. I was going to a home where I would be starting a new life with a man who loved me and had never had to prove that by how quickly he could destroy evidence of drug dealing when cops knocked on the door. Whole new world view!

We walked up the pier together, Hank gripping my hand. Zippy was on our heels, as usual. He trotted behind us, nose in the air, sniffing the breeze with the distant scent of the ocean. The waves sang their splashing cadence along the evenly spaced piles, and an osprey called out from the trees along the shore.

Hank dropped my hand and fiddled with his key in the door, then pushed it open. I was Cinderella walking into the exquisite palace. Newly picked purple coneflowers were arranged in a vase on the small dining room table. (Dining room table!! This was the first dining room table I had ever owned!) White sheer curtains with lace edges graced the kitchen window which looked out directly over the river.

Hank followed me into the small living room where a white wicker loveseat and rocker chair were arranged around a glass top coffee table. Under the glass, shells were artfully placed on a recessed wicker bottom. Light poured in from two big windows on either side of the room.

The hallway led to a bathroom on one side and a bedroom on the other. In both, the theme of white, whicker, and ocean motifs were replicated. The bed had two throw pillows with embroidered dolphins on them.

I was not normally an emotional sort, but seeing those pillows with dolphins did me in. I started sobbing. Not only had I never owned a beautifully embroidered anything, I'd never owned a throw pillow. In fact, until Hank bought me a pillow for my bed in the single wide, I'd never laid my head on a real pillow. My crumpled winter coat usually served that purpose when I'd been growing up.

"What's wrong, Leah?" Hank asked gently. "If the nautical theme doesn't suit you we can change it."

"No, no," I cried, "It's perfect. Perfect. I love it."

He gathered me in his arms, and kissed the top of my head. I repaid his kindness by leaving a big goopy wet spot in the middle of his shirt. Eventually, I pulled myself together, and he asked if I thought I was emotionally able to look at the deck.

I nodded, tears not quite stemmed yet. We walked out the front door and to the side where the major portion of the deck spread out over the river. Two white rocking chairs faced the river with a small end table between them. Another vase of coneflowers adorned the little table.

I sat down in one of the rocking chairs with a deep sigh.

"Please tell your mom it is beautiful."

"I will," he said. "She thought you would like to sit here and work on your writing. A peaceful place for you." He sat down in the other chair and we both rocked in rhythm to the river waves lapping the piles.

Zippy stuck his nose between the deck slats, sniffing. With inexplicable timing, Flash and Pinky rose out of the water, their dorsal fins unmistakable.

"How did they know we were here?" I asked.

Hank shook his head, shrugging. "Maybe there are just a lot of fish here. They do like to hide out in the shade of the deck."

Maybe. However, I don't think it was just an accident. I think they were welcoming me to my new life. I was really glad to see them since one of my unvoiced concerns was they wouldn't visit me in my new home and I would rarely see them. One of the greatest joys of living in my single-wide had been seeing my dolphin friends show up in the mornings, especially at low tide to greet me and catch some breakfast off my shore.

Then, to make the home welcoming even more perfect, an eagle screeched in the distance. We both swung around to look upshore, in the direction of the sound. An eagle perched on a tall pine tree, the upper fifth of which was devoid of needles. All mature Bald Eagles look alike, but my guess is that was Baldy. She shrieked a few more times, swiveling her head to glance all around her, then leveled her gaze on us. At least it looked like she was.

It was completely silent once the eagle settled down. Hank reached over to hold my hand as we rocked and watched the river. Boats rarely came along this section of the river. Most of the people who lived on the river were closer to the gulf or much further north. My section was too marshy to be attractive to home-owners. It was part of the reason I loved this particular stretch of the Suwannee so much.

Basically, people give me the creeps, though Hank feels, with my newfound faith, that will change. He tells me God loves the people He created and so should all who love God. I asked if that applied to the guy they just caught over in Kumsquat Oasis who was peeping in the windows of ladies' bathrooms while they were showering. He told me God doesn't love our sin, but He loves us. I still didn't see how God made that distinction with some of the low-life I have met.

But with the peaceful silence, those sorts of thoughts dissipated.

I was so content that if I closed my eyes, I might have drifted to sleep. In fact, just as my eyes started to slip downward, for the second time that day, the roar of a motorboat going way too fast for the sharp curves in the river filled the silence.

Both Hank and I jumped to our feet and leaned over the deck wondering the same thing. A man was at the helm, a ferocious look smeared across his face. He was scanning the shores, clearly looking for something…or someone.

3

The boat slowed down in time as it rounded the curve beyond our hut. It was shrouded from our sight by the thick reeds but we could hear it, and knew it was right by the trailer home. I prayed silently that Mom and Lolita were out of sight, and that the man would not stop to examine the boat under the tarp.

"I think we covered Lolita's boat just in time," Hank said.

We heard the boat slow as it rounded the hairpin turn in front of my property. The reeds obscured our view of the boat, but it was chugging rather than roaring. He was slowing down and probably looking. I wonder if he thought the covered boat was his. I prayed that Lolita and Mom stayed hidden inside.

We both sighed with relief when we heard the boat rev its engine and roar on its way. There was little doubt the ferocious looking man was the scary boss that Lolita was running from.

My phone rang as we settled back into our rocking chairs. It was Dr. Pritchett, the avian vet. He said Harry the Hawk was getting his wing bandage off today. Dr. Pritchett wanted me there as an "assistant", but also to observe and learn how an expert tackled a bird.

Hank followed me off our precious pier, both of us reluctant to leave. I was happy to learn how to handle injured hawks, but I really couldn't wait to settle into my new home.

"Hope deferred makes the heart sick," Hank said.

"What?"

"It's in the Bible. The end of the verse says: a longing fulfilled is the tree of life."

I had lived most of my life in the hope deferred category. It was going to be good to grab a hold of the tree of life. For now, Hank grabbed a hold of my hand and said he would bring groceries by later and we could cook dinner in our new place. "How does that sound?"

"Like the tree of life," I said, smiling back at him.

Dr. Pritchett was already there by the time we had walked back to the aviary. He stood near Harry's enclosure, gathering supplies.

"New boat?" he asked, tilting his head in direction of the covered motorboat.

"Not ours," I said. "Its owner crashed into our shore this morning."

"Oh my! Is he okay?"

"She," my Mom said, sneaking up on us without us even noticing, which she has a tendency to do. Lolita was a couple of steps behind her.

Dr. Pritchett looked up and almost staggered backwards when he saw Lolita. Mom had helped clean up the blood and bandaged the wound. Lolita had changed into my mom's t-shirt and shorts, and her blond hair was pulled back into a high ponytail. She was barefoot. Even without the outfit that screeched sex appeal like a siren, there was no doubt she was the prettiest lady I had ever seen. I would say from Dr. Pritchett's response I was not the only one that thought so. I honestly didn't know if there was a Mrs. Pritchett or not. I hoped for her sake…not. I'd never seen or heard of a wife, but that didn't mean he didn't have one tucked away somewhere. Our relationship was strictly built on wounded raptors.

With a little awkward sputtering, he expressed thankfulness that she was indeed not too terribly injured. She smiled a devastatingly gorgeous smile and assured him she was fine.

With some difficulty refocusing, Dr. Pritchett told me he would first describe the process and then we would tackle Harry. Mom asked if it was okay if Lolita and she watched, as long as they didn't interfere and stood back out of the way.

Dr. Pritchett nodded, still not in full control of his voice. He forced himself to turn from Lolita and look at Harry the hawk. Harry scowled at him with his hawkish unblinking eyes. Out of the corner of my eye, I could see Lolita leaning forward, watching the hawk and listening to Dr. Pritchett intently.

"Well…so…Leah." Dr. Pritchett cleared his throat. "This is the plan whenever we grab an injured bird the size of a hawk like Harry. If he is facing us as he is now, we will do a front grab. I will reach in with one hand and attempt to restrain both legs simultaneously. Once I have his legs, I will use my other hand to restrain/pin one wing to his body and pull him towards me."

"Won't he grab you with his talons?"

"Good point. I won't pull him too close because his feet are facing me at this point. If he turns, and we grab him from the back, I will reach around with a body grab and pin his wings to the body while trying to reach further and grab one leg in each hand. His wings will be pinned with my forearms, and his feet pointing away from me. His head will not be restrained yet."

"Won't he peck you?"

"Again, good question. Peck is a little tame description of what he might do. Handler safety is important. If at all possible, never leave your face vulnerable – I keep one hand up to protect myself until I have at least one body part under control. Birds recognize the face and some birds will attack (actually it's defense since they are being attacked by you, the predator). Some folks like goggles to protect their eyes."

Here he paused and handed me a pair of goggles. He also had another pair of thick leather gloves that he told me I would need to put on before entering the enclosure.

"Your job as assistant is pretty easy. I mostly want you to just watch. But you will place this light towel over his head once we restrain him. Do that as soon as practical to calm the patient."

I giggled. The use of the word 'patient' tickled me.

"Now when you attempt your first grab, either Mr. Forrest or I will always be nearby with another pair of gloves on so we can reach in and restrain any 'stray' body parts quickly and talk you through the process."

"This sounds dangerous," Lolita chimed in.

Dr. Pritchett turned to look at her, and again the glazed look of a man looking right at the sun swept over his face. "I've done this many times, and no one should try it without training on smaller birds that are less dangerous first. A hawk can't do as much damage as an eagle or a vulture, but he could hurt us if we were not careful."

"I love birds," Lolita said. "I'm named after a bird."

Mom and I stared at her. Since when is there a Lolita bird?

I think Lolita realized she had just clued us in to the fact that Lolita was an alias. Her eyes flicked back and forth, searching for a believable cover. She was adept in her ability to construct lies, however. I will give her that. She quickly added, "My last name is Lark."

Lolita Lark?

Dr. Pritchett nodded. "A lark would be a less dangerous bird to try this on. Of course you have to be careful with small birds…well any bird…but especially small ones. If you hold them too tightly around the body you can harm them and interfere with their breathing."

"That's true of people as well," Lolita said, her voice sad. I am not certain I knew what she meant.

Dr. Pritchett paused, probably recognizing the same wistful note in her voice that I had. "You also need to be careful not to injure them when grabbing the feet. We try to put our middle finger between the two legs so they don't unintentionally cut themselves with their own talons."

"A better use of the middle finger than I'm accustomed to," Lolita said. She didn't even laugh. I don't think she was being crude or joking. She made this observation with a somber expression.

Dr. Pritchett raised an eyebrow, then shook his head a little, turning back to me and the explanation of our imminent bird tackle. "Another important thing to remember is never hold the feet without restraining the rest of the bird. Even a small bird can damage his legs, even break them, with the torque power of flapping wings."

Lolita sighed deeply, and then rubbed her forehead, as though in pain. I wondered if the knock on her head from the accident had caused a concussion. "Poor thing," she said, "Trying to escape his tormentor and he ends up injuring himself??"

Dr. Pritchett scowled. "Well, this is hypothetical, though I have seen it happen in the past. I won't let Harry hurt himself if I can help it. And of course, we are not tormenting the bird…we are trying to help. He doesn't know that however."

"Yes. That is a big difference," she said.

Difference from what? My guess is Lolita was having a whole different conversation in her head than the one we were having. Mom may have had more of a clue than I, because she lay her hand on Lolita's arm and patted her gently.

"So Leah," Dr. Pritchett said, returning us all to the real world and problem in front of us, "Do you have any questions?"

I shook my head. I put on my goggles, pulled on the gloves, and took the small towel I was to use as a head covering once Harry was safely contained. Dr. Pritchett unlatched the enclosure and swooped in so quickly that I was just as surprised as Harry. He grabbed Harry's legs, and in one swift movement, nestled the body and wings against him, and with his other hand, restrained the neck. I hurried in and placed the towel over Harry's head. It was pretty astonishing how calm Harry became with his body so fully restrained now and sight occluded.

At this point, I was just to stand nearby and watch. Dr. Pritchett stretched out Harry's wing but asked me to hold it in that position. He pulled scissors out of his pocket, snipped off the tape binding the wing, and gently removed the bandage. Then he told me to slowly fold the wing back against Harry's side, and leave the enclosure, holding the gate closed.

I did so. Lolita's eyes were wide, watching the whole procedure. In one motion, Dr. Pritchett, settled Harry back on his perch and released his grip on the body while lifting away the head towel. Harry instantly made a quick jab at him, while flapping his wings, but it was more a warning than a full-fledged attack. Dr. Pritchett scurried out of reach, and I latched the gate behind him.

"Wow," Lolita said. "It must feel amazing to help injured birds like that. Such a beautiful bird."

I had to agree with her.

"Harry's going to be just fine," Dr. Pritchett said. "It does feel good when we can help the birds recover. Not as wonderful when we fail."

"Do you fail often?" she asked.

"Not often. Sometimes their injuries are too severe to help them, but usually if they survive the first day we have pretty good odds of returning them to the wild."

"This is work I would enjoy," she said. "Hey, do y'all need help?" She looked at each of us eagerly, swiveling her head like an owl.

"What kind of work did you do before?" Dr. Pritchett asked.

The rest of us looked down, probably all assuming we knew the answer to that, and wondering how honest Lolita would be in her response.

"Customer service," she said.

I didn't dare meet Hank's eyes.

"Right now, Harry is our only customer," I said to break the silence.

Dr. Pritchett nodded. "That's true, though I received a call today from the Florida Raptor center. They have a young injured eagle, a Golden Eagle, that they are bringing over this week. Collided with a car. He'll be with us a few weeks. We never really know when we will have injured birds come in. If you are serious Lolita, we need trained volunteers. Do you live around here?"

"I'm resettling," she said. Her eyes grew watery again, and I feared what terrible secrets might spill out with her tears.

"She'll be staying with me for a while," Mom said, helping ease the grievous memory for Lolita.

Dr. Pritchett, a kind and perceptive man, knew enough to drop that line of questioning. "Leah, and Hank, we will need to cordon off the nest tree from the rest of the aviary. It's possible Tippy and Baldy will already be gone in a week. But if not, they will not take kindly to an injured newcomer sharing their space and we can't shut the nest-end doors."

"Can we shift the tarp as a temporary wall?" Hank asked. It would be easy enough to rig the lines and pulleys to the far end by the tree."

"That's what we were thinking," Dr. Pritchett agreed.

Mom explained to Lolita all about how we raised the eagles, and how the far end of the aviary was built so that the upper portion of the enclosure swung open when the eagle was ready to fly. Honestly, I was surprised both by mom's enthusiasm as she gave an overview of our past few months rehabilitating the eagles, and by Lolita's interest. Lesson learned: Don't judge a book by its 4-inch stilettos or spandex miniskirt.

"What would I do as a volunteer?" she asked.

"Clean the enclosure, catch fish, cut them up for food, prep the hawk food. That's how you start. Slowly, like Leah is learning, you will assist in handling, though not with an eagle. You start with small birds."

"Like larks," I said.

She smiled at me. "I don't know how long I'll be here, but I'd like to help while I am."

"We don't really take in larks," Hank said. "This is a raptor rehab facility."

Dr. Pritchett gathered his supplies and headed back to his car. Hank said he would need to collect materials for the tarp ceiling rope and cable pulley system and followed Dr. Pritchett out. Just Mom, Lolita Lark, and I were left.

There was a moment of silence, then Mom said, "Well now. While there is a break in the excitement, I will go shopping for the wedding dress. Would you like to come, Lolita?"

"Are you getting married?" she asked.

"It's not for me. For Leah."

Lolita looked at me. "You marrying that nice man, Hank, or Dr. Pritchett?" I may have been imagining things, but I think she was worried I had my sights set on Dr. Pritchett. That made me chuckle a bit inside. Dr. Pritchett was old enough to be my father.

"Hank."

She wanted to ask me something else, I am certain, but she pursed her lips and thought better of it. Mom turned to her then and asked again if she'd like to keep her company dress shopping.

"Won't Leah be going with you?" Lolita asked, "I wouldn't want to intrude."

"No. She wants me to pick out her dress. If she had her druthers, she'd get married in the outfit she has on now."

I nodded. That was true.

"Where are you going around here to find a dress?" Lolita asked. She looked worried. I think she was making sure the person she was running away from would not be anywhere near wherever the wedding dress store was.

Mom told her she was starting local – Kumsquat and then Kernersville. If Lolita was familiar with those towns, she probably would have started laughing over the likelihood of snagging a wedding dress in either place. She must have decided she was unlikely to run into the person after her, because she said she'd love to go, and scooted into the trailer to grab her purse.

Sweet Lightning nickered, asking me politely for some scratching behind her ears, and maybe a little bucket of grain if I was so inclined. It wasn't quite her dinner time yet, but close enough. Once I finished tossing her some hay and a few handfuls of grain, I could head back over to my beautiful little hut on the pier.

Mom and Lolita chugged away in the rusty old orange VW. Harry scrutinized me as I stood near Lightning watching her munch her grain with half closed eyes. I wondered how quickly Hank would fix Lolita's boat. Now that I was alone with my thoughts I gave full reign to what I was pretty sure was her story.

She was either an official 'escort' of some rich man or a prostitute. She probably stole the boat, in my opinion, and that's why she didn't want us calling the police. On the other hand, the source of the fear she definitely displayed was possibly because, whoever the man that she was running from, he either had hurt her or would hurt her if he caught up to her. Considering my background, I was inclined to give folks the benefit of the doubt. I liked Lolita, even if I didn't entirely approve of her profession. If I was right about her profession. I'd bet the rent I *was* right.

Now I know what you are thinking. Were we crazy to house a total stranger, probably a hooker, who likely did steal a boat, and was running from either the law or someone who was dangerous and in pursuit of this stranger?

Yes. We were. No doubt. But before you start lecturing, let me share what I had JUST read the night before Lolita crashed into my life. Like I told you earlier, I was a brand new Christian. I was determined to find out more about this crazy leap of faith I had just made. So when the sun set, and the moon was about a third of the way through its arc over the Suwannee river, I nestled in bed and popped open my Bible. I was reading through the Bible in order, very slowly. However, I also liked to flip randomly to different books to get a flavor of what was to come since I was still slogging through one of the less exciting books in the Old Testament called Numbers. The name should be all you need to know to understand why I wasn't eating up the words like they were candy.

Anyway, I had flipped to this section: Jeremiah 30:17 *For I will restore health to you, and your wounds I will heal, declares the LORD, because they have called you an outcast: 'It is Zion, for whom no one cares!'*

I read that verse over and over. It really struck me for several reasons. First, I had a whole lot of wounds from my past that had needed healing. They weren't physical wounds, but that didn't make them any less painful. Probably made them even more painful! Secondly, I had been an outcast, doomed from birth by parents who loved drugs and drink more than their daughter. And finally, I knew what it was to feel all alone, damaged and despairing, whom no one cared about.

When I saw Lolita, I saw a kindred spirit. I didn't need to know her story. Whatever she had been through to bring her crashing to my shore, it had not been easy. I felt that as surely as I felt God was speaking directly to me in that passage of

Jeremiah. And maybe part of His message was this—I have restored you. Now help restore Lolita Lark.

4

I had just finished cutting up a mouse for Harry's dinner when I heard the familiar sound of the dolphins surfacing just off my shore. I washed my hands and hurried to the water. The entire pod of four were there – Flash, Pinky, Mama, and No-Name. It was not like me to falter with names but No-Name was not around very often, and we weren't sure of his connection to the others. Flash and Mama were an item, and the parents of Pinky. No-Name may have been Pinky's boyfriend, or maybe it was the Grandpa. Since he didn't come around as often as the others, I felt no huge rush to name him. Hank thought No-Name was catchy.

Now I sat on the edge of the shoreline with my toes in the water. Flash surfaced and made some clicking sounds, his version of "How's it going?" The others were intent on fishing and didn't even bother to say hello. I loved watching the dolphins. I could do that all day, and sometimes did. When the current was strong, they would line up facing the flow and remain stationary for minutes at a time. I guess they were underwater with their mouths wide open, letting the fish float right down their esophagus. I don't know that for sure, but I think it is a good guess.

Right now, they bobbed up and down in a wide circle. I had left Lightning's gate open so she could join me by the water and she was making her way towards me slowly, nibbling at the slim pickings along the shore. Flash raised his snout out of the water again and called to her. "Eheheheheh!"

I had heard dolphins make that noise before, but it wasn't till I had my own dolphin and horse friends that I realized how similar it sounded to a horse's nicker. Lightning answered, as she usually did with a matching cadence. Then she lifted her head, ears perked, staring fixedly upstream.

The motorboat I had seen earlier in the day with the gruff looking man was returning. He drove at a much slower pace and closer to shore. The hair on my arms raised, and I wished Hank were back. To my horror, he slowed even more as he neared my shore. The dolphins disappeared.

"Howdy," he called, idling his boat right across the river from me.

I nodded at him, but didn't speak, hoping he would go away.

"Not many folks on the river these parts," he said.

"No. There never are," I said.

He looked at the covered boat and then pointed. "Why aren't you out on your boat on a nice day like this?" His words were friendly enough, but his face did not match the companionable chit-chat.

"Needs repair," I said.

He nodded, eyes running over the tarp as though he could see through it. I assume if it was his boat, he might recognize the outlines draped by the cover. Hopefully it was a common boat type. All motorboats looked alike to me, but I wasn't much of an expert. His boat drifted closer. Lightning laid her ears back which she only did when she was picking up dangerous vibes.

I think the man was considering coming ashore but two things dissuaded him. First, the sound of his voice must have finally roused Zippy from whatever patch of sun he was lounging in, and he came racing to the bank, barking and growling. Second, Hank's truck had just rolled up the gravel driveway. I'm always glad to see Hank, but was especially glad now.

When Hank got out of his truck and waved, the man in the motorboat returned the wave briefly and turned back downstream. Before Hank had even reached my side, the hull of his boat was slapping against the waves and zooming out of sight.

"Looks like the same boat we saw earlier," Hank said.

"I think it is whoever Lolita is running from."

Hank nodded, forehead wrinkled with concern. I knew what he was thinking, because I was thinking it too. If Lolita stole the boat, we were harboring a criminal. Fortunately, I am good friends with a cop and if there was a stolen boat reported, he would know about it. I unpocketed my cellphone and called

William. I wasn't totally upfront with him, since I had told Lolita we would not call the police. Just in case she was an innocent victim, I thought it best to stick to minimal disclosure.

"Hey William," I said when he answered, "We met a pretty strange man in a motorboat just now. Never have seen him on the river before, and he was asking about boats along shore. Any stolen boats been reported?"

"Stolen boats? No. Not around here. Did he say someone had stolen his boat?"

"No…not exactly, but he was asking questions. I had the feeling he was looking for a boat."

"What did he ask?"

I probably should have had my story a little more carefully worked out. I didn't want to lie to William, and on top of that, Hank was listening. I had a feeling he wouldn't approve of me stretching the truth. I didn't want William snooping around here till we knew the scoop on Lolita.

"I don't remember exactly," I said. "Oh, gotta go. Hank just showed up with a bunch of work we have to do on the aviary." William asked a few other questions, puzzled by my call, but I finally managed to confuse him enough that he said he would check into any reported boat thefts and get back to me.

I turned off my phone, without looking at Hank.

"So, what did that man in the boat say?" Hank asked.

"He said there weren't many people on the river. I think he was fishing for me to tell him I'd seen Lolita on the river. And he was looking real hard at the boat under the tarp. I think if you hadn't come when you did, he might have anchored right here and lifted the tarp."

"No stolen boats according to William?"

I shook my head.

He opened his mouth, and I am pretty sure he was about to give me a gentle lecture on telling the truth, the whole truth, and nothing but the truth, but Mom's VW chugged up the drive in the nick of time. I hadn't really cared at all about the wedding dress, but it was the perfect opportunity to forego the lesson on 'thou shalt not lie'.

Mom and Lolita hopped out, no packages in hand.

"No wedding dress?" I asked, glad for the diversion.

Mom held out her empty arms. "We scoured every store in Kernersville. Found some great deals on manure but not a single wedding dress in the whole town."

"You may need to take a trip to Orlando," Hank suggested.

"A man in a boat came by," I said to Lolita. "I wondered if he was looking for someone."

Lolita grimaced. "What did he look like?"

"Big. Receding brown hair. Kind of gruff voice."

"What color was his boat?" she asked.

"White. I think it had a red stripe."

"Did he ask about me?"

"No…he asked if many people were on the river though. And he took a long time looking at the tarped boat."

"He wouldn't know that boat," she said, nodding towards the damaged boat on shore.

Hank glanced at me. She didn't seem worried about the boat being recognized. Maybe she really didn't steal it. Whatever her situation, she didn't share it now.

"If you want to show me what you do to feed the hawk, I'd like to watch," she said. I don't think she was just changing the subject. She said it with a hopeful lilt in her voice.

"I'll get our own dinner going," Mom said. "I've seen enough diced up mouse bits to last me a month."

As Mom headed to the house, Hank told her not to expect us for dinner. We were going to have a feast at the fishing hut. She raised an eyebrow, but didn't comment. I have no doubt she thought Hank would be staying at the fishing hut with me overnight. Maybe you do too. Get those dirty thoughts out of your head. Hank was a normal man, but he had made it clear that he was strictly by the book when it came to sex outside of marriage. And I mean by *THE* BOOK.

I remember that discussion. Shortly after we were engaged, Hank wanted me to know that sexual purity was very important to him because it was important to God.

"God cares about that?" I asked.

"He made Adam and Eve man and wife before they conceived Cain."

"Did she wear a wedding dress?" I asked. I was joking, since I knew their first clothes were fig leaves… but Hank answered me seriously.

"The Bible doesn't mention that," Hank said, "But it does say in Genesis 3:6 that Adam was the husband of Eve."

"Was there some sort of official ceremony?" I asked.

This may not seem very important to you, but I was trying to find any way to wiggle out of the fancy affair of a formal wedding.

"If there was, it isn't mentioned. Though I guess you don't get any more official than being joined together in the presence of God Himself."

Then he gripped my hand. "That's why I want to be married by a Pastor, a man of God. It's very important to me that we be made man and wife by an official devoted to God with vows made before God."

That may shed some light on why I was submitting to the fancy dress, official wedding, and all the hoopla. Hank never asked for anything, but this mattered to him…so it mattered to me.

All that is to say, Mom may have her doubts about Hank being a gentleman and not breaking any standards of conduct in the privacy of the fishing hut, but not me. My virginity was safe. If you are hoping for porn, you need to look elsewhere.

Lolita clapped her hands together. "Diced mouse bits?" she asked.

"That's what we feed Harry. Come on, I'll show you."

"I'll just put the supplies for the aviary tarp pulley by the shed," Hank said. "That way it will be ready to go for the morning."

Lolita followed me into our new 'medical building'. It was the size of a large shed but had a few cages along the side wall for any new 'patients' that weren't healthy enough for the outside enclosure.

I pulled the diced mouse bits out of the fridge and measured a small amount into the feeding bowl. I added some antibiotics to those appetizing tidbits, and stirred it in. Then we headed back to Harry's enclosure. I slid open the little feeding door right by a shelf along the wall, and placed the bowl on the shelf.

"That's all there is to that," I said.

"How many times a day do you feed Harry?" Lolita said, "That looks easy enough and I would like to repay you all for putting me up for a few days."

"Twice," I said. "I'll be back in the morning if you want to help. The instructions are written on the refrigerator door dry erase board, but I could watch while you do it."

"Ok," she said. "I'd like that."

We stepped back, and watched Harry hop over to the shelf. He glanced at us, but seemed satisfied we were not going to disturb him and dug into his dinner, peering at us between bites.

"Your mom told me a little about your childhood, Leah."

I turned slowly to Lolita. That would not have been a cheery story.

"I know a little of what you went through," she said. "I had a similar upbringing except my dad beat me...and...worse."

"I'm sorry," I said. What creepy evil existed in the midst of such a beautiful world!

"I have to say I am impressed by how well you treat your mother given your history."

"That wasn't always true," I said.

"I can't imagine it was easy to forgive."

"No."

"What made you able to do that...to forgive?"

"I'm not totally sure. It was a long process. A couple of years. I guess the only thing I know for sure was when I became a Christian, I understood forgiveness a little better."

She was quiet, watching Harry gobbling his food. With each bite, he swiveled his head to assure himself we were keeping our distance.

"The only one I am less likely to forgive than my father is God," Lolita said.

Her eyes were tight pinpricks of anger. Her fists clenched as though to squeeze the memory and pain away. I recognized the gesture. Maybe it is common to people with crappy childhoods. I knew that Hank would talk about God in some comforting way, but I could not for the life of me come up with a single thing to say.

Except this: "I understand."

She leaned against the aviary wall, which earned her an angry snap of Harry's head to watch her. Aware of his distress, she stepped back. "I imagine you do. So what made you become a Christian? Did you ever wonder why God allowed your parents to put you through such hell?"

"Yes. Honestly, I can't tell you that I have come up with any good answer to that."

"So you are giving God a pass on destroying your childhood?"

I looked at her, pondering the question. Had I?

"Maybe," I said finally. "But it didn't really feel that way. I just became grateful for what He brought me when I made it out of my past. When I came here."

"To the abandoned trailer? Your mom told me it wasn't quite the 'treasure' it is now."

"No. It was pretty decrepit. No water or electricity. No door even. But right away, Lightning showed up. She's not a typical horse. She's more like my best friend. And then the dolphins…"

"They are not so typical either."

"Right. And then Zippy was thrown off a boat to drown, and Flash, the dolphin, saved him. Brought him to me. It was like God was sending me all these messages that I was not alone or too wretched to save."

"Did you think it was God sending the animals?"

"Not then. I do now. Then I thought it was that misfits attract each other. We were a sorry skinny bunch. Then I met Hank."

Lolita smiled. "He seems to worship the ground you walk on."

"I don't know about that, but he loves God. He was the first person I ever met that made me feel I was someone special."

"I wonder what that feels like," Lolita said. She brushed a strand of hair across her forehead and winced. She must have hit the bashed area of her head.

"It was like landing in a foreign country," I told her. Not that I'd ever done that. But I bet landing in a foreign country would be completely outside everything you were used to. Hank's kindness was maybe the first gentleness I'd ever experienced.

I really wanted to question Lolita about her life. What had happened to her when her abusive dad finally lost his grip on her? How had she escaped? She hadn't landed in a pleasant place like I had. That was for sure.

She didn't volunteer any information, and I didn't want to pry. She pressed her fingers against her eyes, like she was in pain.

"It's good you found safety while you were still young. Before too much happened that rusted all your shiny spots."

"Hank always told me that nothing was so broken that God could not restore it," I told her.

"Well I admire Hank's sunny outlook," Lolita said, her words crisp and bitter. "My head is aching like a vise is squeezing my skull. I'm gonna go lie down. I appreciate all your help. You just wake me up when you are ready to feed Harry if I'm not out yet. You can show me whatever else you need me to do with the animals. I want to help. To thank you."

She spun around and headed to the front door of the trailer. As she rounded the corner, Lightning was ambling down the field on the way to remind me it was time for her grain and hay. Lolita stopped in front of the horse. Lightning lowered her nose blowing warm air onto Lolita's arm. Lolita slowly lifted her hand and rubbed her palm down the white blaze of Lightning's forehead. Lightning stood still, and even from several yards away, I could hear her unspoken message. It will be okay. She'd whispered it to me enough times.

5

Hank made a stupendous creamy chicken casserole with linguine for our maiden dinner in our new home. We sat at the dining room table, which would have been excitement enough for me. Real food made by my future husband was just icing on the cake. Literally, by the way. He also made a cake and made the icing from scratch! I didn't even know that was possible. (Don't judge me until you have walked a mile in my shoes. Which were usually three sizes too small and dredged out of a garbage dump.)

"Hank," I said, licking the chocolate molecules off my fork dreamily, "Do you think I should learn how to cook once we are married?"

"It *is* a useful skill," he said.

"I'm sorry I never really learned how," I said, feeling very sad for Hank. "Maybe you haven't fully considered what you are getting yourself into by marrying me."

"Cooking is easy," he said. "Anyone can learn to cook. Not everyone can learn to survive in the wild, making a fishing net from reeds and catching shrimp for dinner."

He was referring to my first few weeks squatting in the abandoned trailer with no money, no job, few clothes, and nothing approaching ready-made dinners. I had indeed made a fishing net out of reeds and the busted screen from the old trailer. I cooked the shrimp over a fire for many weeks, until I managed to get a job and upgraded to canned ravioli. Until that point, I had survived mostly on candy bars. Snitched from the Kumsquat Oasis Camping Store, I am sorry to admit.

I agreed that anyone could learn to cook, however. My mom was a case in point. She had never shown any interest in the culinary arts when I was a kid. Peanut butter sandwiches were as gourmet a meal as I recall us ever being served. However, since she had moved in with me a year or so ago, she had become a passably decent cook, and always made our meals. That's why thus far, I had never needed to develop any more expertise than heating canned food which is all I lived on till she moved in.

For some reason, despite the fact that Hank never made me feel guilty about anything, I knew this was something most wives knew how to do, and I should do everything in my power to accomplish.

"Tomorrow, I will cook you a real dinner," I said. "If you decide you want to take back the marriage offer afterwards, I will totally understand."

He grinned at me. "And the hut?"

"No. I keep the hut no matter what." I drew my eyebrows together in the most menacing face I could muster to show I was serious.

"What will you make?"

"Probably a disaster…What would you suggest?"

"Start simple. How about broiled chicken, baked potato, and a salad? Those are all pretty easy."

I jotted those in my memory. I'd google instructions later when Hank was gone. I had learned how to build an eagle nest and most of what I needed to know to raise little Tippy from orphaned eaglet to fledgling using the internet. Broiling a chicken couldn't be harder than that!

I put the dishes in the sink and told Hank I would wash them later. For now, I wanted to sit with him on our dock, watching the sun set. He agreed and said maybe one day we could get a dishwasher.

"I may not know how to cook," I said, "But I have been washing dishes since I was four. I excel in dishwashing."

This was true too. We may have only had peanut butter sandwiches to eat, but they were always served on real plates. We only had three, one for each of us, and I used to enjoy washing the plates. They had pretty designs on them. In the winter, the hot water on my hands was the only warmth I would enjoy for the day. It was not exactly the world's cushiest childhood, but even in all the squalor of my life, I managed to find those high points. Mom used to threaten me by saying I wouldn't be allowed to wash the dishes if I didn't shape up.

We settled onto the beautiful white rocking chairs and rocked in cadence with the waves lapping at the reeds along the shore. A great blue heron skimmed over the water and then flapped his enormous wings and settled a little further downstream in a shallow eddy. He froze, slowly coiled his neck back, and then darted his long sharp bill into the shallows. A fish was speared on his bill, still wriggling and trying to escape. With lightning fast movements, he tossed the fish into his mouth, snapped his sharp beak around it and walked with his stiff legged, stately steps into the reeds towards a hidden spit of shore to eat his prize.

"Did you learn anything more about Lolita?" Hank asked.

"Not much. Her father was a creep…even worse than mine. She didn't tell me much about her life now. She's mad at God."

Hank nodded. Zippy had followed us out to the deck, and now curled up beside Hank. Hank reached over, scratching the little sleeping dog.

"Hank, why do you think God lets evil people prey on children like that?"

Hank rocked, looking out over the water. "I can't answer that, Leah."

We had had this discussion in different ways several times since I'd known Hank. It was one of those sticking points for me that kept me from embracing the whole God-business for a long time. I still had no good answer. I wish I did. I'm not sure how I managed to stumble into belief and faith with that unanswered elephant trumpeting in the room.

"If this life was all there is, that would be a show-stopper for me," Hank said, mirroring my thoughts.

"But for someone who doesn't know God, this life is all there is," I said. "At least that's what they believe. Why would God create someone only to have them suffer through no fault of their own? Lolita couldn't help being born to a monster."

"I don't know," Hank repeated. "There are for sure things I don't know, and can't know. So, I focus instead on what I *do* know. I know that God created the universe because nothing else makes sense to me. I know He created the earth and every person that inhabits it. I know He created beauty, and joy, and provided all that was necessary for abundant life. And He gave us free will so we could choose to love Him or not for all He is and for all He created. I know that even Satan began as 'an angel of light' and then his own pride and desire challenged God's authority which led to great evil. I know that God in His mercy gave us a way back to Him through Jesus, and that way was filled with suffering. Why suffering became the vehicle to eternal life…I don't know. It is not what I would have chosen if I were God. But it would never have been necessary if rebellion against God had not been permitted. Sorry for the sermon. I have thought a lot about this…"

That was a lot to absorb, so I munched on those thoughts silently.

"But it's hard to tell someone who has seen only suffering about God's goodness," Hank admitted.

I thought of the beautiful plates from my childhood and how wonderful it felt to wash them in the warm soapy water as my frozen fingers thawed.

"Maybe I should make a shopping list," I said.

Hank cocked his head, and laughed. "To help Lolita learn about God's goodness?"

"No…to be sure I have everything I need to make dinner tomorrow."

I only had a vague idea of something called a broiler pan. I hoped I would be able to recognize it if I saw it in the drawer under the stove. I hated to show the full extent of my ignorance to my future groom. Despite the aversion to the wedding dress and the overwhelming ceremony, I would hate to lose Hank over something as simple as a broiling pan. I'd google it as soon as Hank left.

"Think about this," Hank said, "If you know that something is evil, that really could be an argument *for* God instead of against Him."

"How?"

"Well, on what basis do you call it evil?"

I shook my head. "It just is. It's obvious that it is not good."

"That's because you have a standard of what *is* good. If you didn't have that standard, how could you call anything evil?"

Frankly, it was easier just to worry about the problem of broiling pans.

"How did any of us determine what was good or bad…unless the moral standard which we all recognize is put in place first? And who put it there?"

"God is what you're hunting for… but why didn't God just make a world without evil?"

"He could have. In fact, if He just created nothing, there would be no possibility of evil."

"Well…yes. But then you wouldn't be here, or me…or Zippy and Lightning. What fun is there in that?"

"I agree. So God created something, and if God is all righteous, holy, and good, then what He created was good. But if He didn't give His creation the choice to choose good or not good, then He just created robots."

"Again, not much fun."

"No…and the Bible says that God created us because He loved us, and His desire is for us to love and follow Him. But not because He has forced us to. If you had no choice but to marry me, that wouldn't be much of a choice, would it?"

"No, but I'd make it anyway!"

"It wouldn't mean as much to me if you married me because I was the only man on earth."

I thought of William Spear, the cop. He had wanted to date me when Hank and I were not yet an official item. I had made a choice for Hank. I wondered if Hank knew that. At the time, I'd kept the turmoil in my heart hush-hush, and I suspected that is where it ought to remain.

"So before I get too tangled in my own thoughts, what I am saying is God must be good because we have a standard of good. He didn't create evil…He just created the choice to turn from Good, from Him. And that started the whole ball of sin rolling when Satan was able to deceive Adam and Eve into questioning God's goodness."

"So what would you say to Lolita when she says the only one she can forgive less than her evil father is God?"

Hank looked at me and finally shrugged. "I don't know. For now, I guess I would say I understand. But maybe then I would try to show her God's goodness *now*. I suspect there are few people more able to help her through that than you."

"Me? I haven't even worked my way through the first four books of the Bible."

"There's a verse in the Bible, 2 Corinthians 1:4. It says: *God comforts us in all our affliction, so that we may be able to comfort those who are in any affliction, with the comfort with which we ourselves are comforted by God.*"

"You think God sent me my lousy parents so I could help Lolita sort through why He sent her lousy parents?"

"Not quite. I think that the comfort and forgiveness you found through God in spite of your struggles may be able to help Lolita."

I nodded, but what I was thinking, truth be told, was this was a much taller order than figuring out how to broil the chicken.

6

The next morning, by the time I arrived at Harry's cage to feed him, Lolita was already there waiting for me. Her hair was pulled back in a ponytail. No make-up. Mom's old t-shirt and baggy shorts completed the ensemble. She looked almost like a normal beautiful woman rather than an exponentially off the charts *spectacularly* beautiful woman.

"Good morning," she said. "I slept like the dead last night. I don't know when I have slept more deeply. Maybe never."

"I felt the same way when I came here," I said. "I think the river sounds are like a lullaby."

"Yes…with the white noise of your mother's snores."

I laughed. Maybe that was why the hut had seemed so quiet last night!

"I heard an owl, and the eagles."

"They don't get along," I said.

"It is a beautiful peaceful place. I'm glad I crashed here."

Harry watched us from his perch. By now, he knew me and associated me with food. He was more wary than usual. Lolita must have concerned him. I led her to the medical shed, and showed her the instructions written on the white board regarding Harry's feeding and care instructions. After pointing out where the mouse bits were, and the antibiotics, I leaned back against the wall and watched her measure Harry's breakfast and meds into a small feeding bowl. Then I showed her how to slide open the feeding door to his enclosure and hook the bowl next to the ledge near his perch.

"That's it," I said. "He's pretty easy now. When he first came, it was a lot more work. Now, we just feed twice a day and clean his cage. Once a week when Dr. Pritchett comes to check his wing and his leg, I clean out the enclosure. Dr. Pritchett lets me help a little with catching him. It will be a while before I get to do that myself."

"This is what you want to do for a living?" Lolita asked.

"For now. I like being near animals…and birds."

She dipped her chin slowly in agreement. "They are a lot nicer than most people."

I thought this was the perfect opening to ask her about her job, but couldn't bring myself to open that can of worms.

"I thought maybe I'd go into marine biology, but then the eagle stuff just fell in my lap…and I didn't really want to leave here even for two years to get my degree."

"Your mom told me you write books."

"A little. I wrote two books and the publisher liked them. They pay me enough to keep me interested in writing more but not enough to live on."

"What does Hank do?"

"He works in construction, but he wants to become a Fish and Wildlife Service officer like his dad."

"Living around here, you probably don't need much money," Lolita observed, turning slowly and taking in the view of the swampy shore.

"I lived on practically nothing," I said.

"How does Dr. Pritchett survive?" she asked. "I can't imagine taking care of injured hawks is enough to earn much of a living or support a family."

"I never heard him mention family," I said. Her interest in Dr. Pritchett was obvious and I couldn't stand to see her suffer casting about for information. "But I know he travels pretty far as an avian vet. He has a regular veterinary practice as well."

Dr. Pritchett was a good bit older than me, so I had never really considered him as attractive or not. But now, as I pondered the lovely Lolita's interest in him, I could understand it. He was a shy, unassuming man, quiet. His eyes were dark and soulful, and his features regular with a strong chin anchoring his face. Tall and toned from all his work with animals and being outdoors. Yes. I could see the attraction.

Lightning interrupted our discussion with a shrill neighing. She had waited as long as she planned to for her breakfast. Lolita tagged along behind me, saying she might be here a while. Best to learn how to help with all the chores. When I opened the gate to Lightning's pasture, she butted her muzzle against me a little harder than was necessary. I think she was expressing her displeasure in waiting while we lollygagged with the hawk and chit-chat over Lolita's interest in Dr. Pritchett. I told her, "Hold your horses, Miss Impatience!" which made Lolita laugh.

It sure didn't take much to tickle Lolita's funny bone. Maybe she hadn't had much opportunity for laughter in her "customer service" job.

I showed her how to shake out three flakes of hay for Lightening and give her a scoop of grain in her bucket. Then I showed her where the hose spigot was and how to fill Lightning's water trough.

Just then, Dr. Pritchett screeched into our driveway. He was more than his usual amount of flustered as he told us that he had two injured raptors all dazed and doped up in cages back at his office that would be moving in to our rehab center…if they survived.

"With the golden eagle coming next week, and these patients, you are about to have a full house," Dr. Pritchett said.

While we were standing there watching the water swirl and absorbing this latest news, we heard a resounding smack. We all snapped our heads around just in time to see a robin slam into the back window of the mobile home and crash to the ground.

Lolita rushed to the weedy ground beneath the window, and fished out the stunned robin. She cradled him in her hands and brought him to Dr. Pritchett. The robin blinked, so I knew it was alive, but it didn't move otherwise.

"I hope its neck isn't broken," she said.

As if on cue, the robin looked up at her.

"I don't think it is," Dr. Pritchett said. "It probably just has a really bad headache. May I?"

He offered his cupped hands next to Lolita's. She carefully transferred the robin into his hands. He gently gripped the little robin around the chest and then spread one wing slowly. Then shifting his hold, he did the same to the other.

"I don't think there is a break," he said. "I think we just put this little guy down and watch him."

He returned the robin to the shade by the house, near where he had had his kamikaze collision. He stepped back slowly, while we all watched. The robin shook his head. Then with a swift practice flap of his wings, he spread them in earnest and before we quite knew what he was up to, he was lost in the upper branches of the nearby tree.

"You healed him!" Lolita said, a worshipful expression draped over her perfect features.

"God healed him," Dr. Pritchett said, laughing, "All I did was let him know he was ok."

This bit of profound insight caught me by surprise. Given all my recent thoughts about God, forgiveness, and psychic healing, his words struck a chord.

"I didn't see God," Lolita said.

Dr. Pritchett cocked his head, looking at her sadly.

"So, we need to get another enclosure ready. Our new patients are a mother and juvenile Red Shoulder Hawk. They were hit by a train."

I did a double take. Hit by a train? Now that is not something you expect a bird to run into.

"That doesn't happen often," Dr. Pritchett said, "But it is not unheard of. Trains tend to travel through isolated areas where hawks hunt."

"How badly are they hurt?"

"We'll know more if they last the night," Dr. Pritchett said. "Both have a bruised or broken hip, broken wing, head injuries, and possibly…probably…internal injuries."

"Poor things," Lolita said.

"I'll help you set up the new enclosure now, but another heads-up. The golden eagle from Florida Rehab will be arriving soon, along with Tim, a rehab worker who will be training you and helping with the eagle. They do not expect the golden eagle to be with us long, and thought this would be a good time to have you shadow an expert."

Lolita looked like she was ready to pop. Finally, she burst open. "I am looking for new work. Can I shadow him too?"

Dr. Pritchett sputtered. "Well, you are welcome to observe as well, Lolita, and help as he directs. But there are only enough funds for one employee, and that's pretty meager."

I could attest to the meager funds. I wasn't paid much, but it was enough for my needs.

"That's all right," she said. "I will volunteer. Maybe one day there will be enough work for two."

"There will be enough work…just not enough money," he said. "Always the problem. But there is plenty to learn. Tim will be bringing some dead birds to teach you some of the things you need to learn."

"Dead birds?" I said, feeling a little sick.

"Raptors that didn't make it."

"Won't they…smell bad?" Lolita asked.

"They are refrigerated."

"What kind of skills?"

"Giving injections, the physical exam, eye exam, physical therapy, bandage and wound care…That sort of thing. I know you have seen me do some of those things, Leah, but you can learn a lot from practicing on a dead bird. And you won't have to worry about killing it while you learn."

"Sounds fun!" Lolita said. I was not as fully convinced as she was.

"While I am here, I also have some materials for you to study. Now that the crisis with the eagles is over and they are likely to fly off for good any day, I'd like to start you researching the different birds we are likely to encounter and start learning as much as you can about them."

That sounded more enticing than handling refrigerated raptors.

"For now, let's take a look at the hawk enclosure and see what we will need in there for our new patients."

Harry watched us, shifting to the far corner of his cage as we entered the adjoining enclosure. There was only one perch in the empty enclosure. Dr. Pritchett said the mother and juvenile would be housed together, but it was best to install another perch.

"I will need to talk to Hank about the other modification. We don't want to be traveling through all the enclosures each time we want to get to the golden eagle area so I will have Hank cut a new door right here."

He pointed to a section of the long wall that was in the middle segment of the aviary. "And this area will need three perches at varying heights. I have the two smaller ones in the van. Between the three of us, we can probably get those dug in and ready. For the tallest one we'll need Hank and Mr. Forrest to help."

I glanced at Lolita. My guess, judging from her neatly manicured and polished fingernails, was that she had not done a whole lot of digging in the dirt in her lifetime. She surprised me by clapping her perfect hands together and saying, "Goody!"

Dr. Pritchett showed us where he wanted us to start digging post holes. He was fully prepared. His van not only housed the perches, but also three shovels.

The benefit of living on a floodplain of the Suwannee river is if you ever need to dig a hole, you have very soft dirt you have to blast through. Even Lolita, who I would wager had never shoveled even one shovel-full of dirt, had little trouble with the hole she was put in charge of. When the holes were done, and the perches balanced in the holes, Dr. Pritchett mixed up some quick cement and dumped it in the holes. Then we helped him pound in stakes to either side of each perch and tie them in a vertical position.

It was lunch time by the time the three perches we could install were all ready with the cement drying and solidifying around them. Lolita held out her hands, showing us blisters and three cracked fingernails.

"Sorry," Dr. Pritchett said.

"For what? I haven't had this much fun in years."

Now I will admit it was satisfying to step back and see the fruit of our labor, but *fun?*

Dr. Pritchett rewarded her with an admiring smile. It was a different look he gave her than the time when he first saw her, and it looked like his eyebrows were about to be scorched by the heat of her dazzling beauty. I think she noticed. I suspect it was rare men looked at her without drool dripping out of their mouths.

Hank's truck rumbled around the bend in the road, and now rolled down my driveway, coming to a stop alongside Dr. Pritchett's van.

I guess Dr. Pritchett had already warned him about the door he needed to install because he hopped out and started unloading sawhorses, saws, hammers, nails, and plywood.

"You're just in time," Dr. Pritchett said, "I was just going to take these ladies to lunch for all their hard work. Want to join us?"

"Thanks, but no. I have another job this afternoon. I would just as soon get this door installed right away."

"I'll stay and keep Hank company," I said. "Who knows? Maybe I can learn how to operate the power saw."

"Well I'm starving," Lolita said.

Dr. Pritchett looked a little scared, if you ask me. My guess is he liked Lolita as much as she liked him, but knew she was out of his league. Still, he gestured towards his car, and said he couldn't promise anything fancy in Kumsquat, but she was welcome to join him. First, he pulled out a pile of books and handed them to me.

"The list of birds and study questions is in the top notebook," he said.

I gathered the books in my arms.

"Have fun," I said.

Lolita winked at me as she hopped into the car. She tucked her red painted toes inside the cab just as the same boat we'd seen the day before came trolling around the bend in the river. Lolita saw it as soon as we did. It had approached with little warning, the engine idling as the scowling driver moved slowly along the shore. Lolita slumped inside the truck, though I'm sure the boat driver could not see her with the sun reflecting off the windshield. It was clear she recognized the driver and did not want to be seen.

Hank whispered something to Dr. Pritchett who immediately backed out. Then Hank approached the shore, waving in a friendly manner. Knowing Hank, I knew he was not feeling nearly as friendly as he appeared.

"You looking for something?" he called to the driver.

"Fish," the man said.

"Having any luck?"

"Hoping it's about to change." That sounded menacing to me, though it could have been my imagination.

"Saw you yesterday," Hank said. "You new around here?"

"Just on vacation," he said. His smile was not the slightest bit warm.

"I figured," Hank said. "I been here a long time and I never forget a face."

This was a warning. I don't know if the boat driver knew it, but I knew it. Hank was not smiling when he said it either. He was giving a clear message.

The driver peered at Hank, the fake smile gone. Message received. He gunned the engine and the boat spurted to life and disappeared around the next bend.

"She knew him," I said to Hank. He nodded.

"I can only help a little while," I told Hank. "I have to pick up the things I need to make you dinner and then…make it. How long should I plan on this whole project taking?"

"The door?"

"No…the chicken and the baked potato."

He laughed, and then unexpectedly enveloped me in a hug. "Count on an hour for the potato to bake, and the chicken can broil in thirty minutes."

"Broil and bake are two different things though." I knew that from the brief research I'd been able to conduct the night before, right before drifting off to sleep.

"Yes," Hank said. If he was inclined to make fun of me, he repressed it. One of the many reasons I loved Hank was he never tried to get a laugh at someone else's discomfort or expense.

"So how do I have them come out hot at the same time?"

"That's always the hardest part about cooking. I bake the potato first and let it stay in the oven while you broil the chicken. Keep it on the bottom shelf. It won't overcook but should stay warm wrapped in the foil with the broiler going."

"How did you learn all this?" I asked.

"When Mom got sick, and Dad was out working long hours, I became the family chef," he said.

I put my hand on his arm gently.

He put his own calloused hand over mine.

"It was ok. I liked to cook, and that way I could have whatever I felt like eating for dinner."

"Were you mad at God for making your mother sick?"

Hank shook his head slowly. "I never thought it was God who made her sick."

"But God is in control of all things."

"Yes. But sin has corrupted the entire world. There was no disease in Eden."

"He could have stopped diseases."

"Yes."

"Are you angry that He didn't…at least in your mom?"

He paused before answering. I think Hank worried that if he answered my questions wrong, my new faith would shatter. He may have been right about that.

"I wasn't angry so much as sad. I didn't want her to be sick, and of course we all prayed, and still do, for her healing."

"Do you ever wonder why God doesn't answer that prayer?"

"Well, so far His answer is not to heal her. It's not the answer I want, and maybe it is not the final answer, but it doesn't mean He hasn't answered."

"That seems cruel."

"Yes, it does. But things are not always as they seem."

I really loved yet another thing about Hank. He never tried to pretend he knew what he didn't know. He also never made me feel foolish for the stupid questions I asked.

"So why don't you believe God is cruel when He seems cruel?"

"Well, I didn't say God seems cruel but the fact that she is not healed by Him seems cruel."

"Isn't that the same thing?"

"Maybe, but I don't think so. It is not at all what I want or what any of my family wants. But there are good things that have come of it."

I shook my head, forehead wrinkled in disbelief. "Like what???"

"Like for one, I know how to broil chicken and bake potatoes…and I can teach you," he said smiling. "For another, a lot of families rip each other apart and nit-pick over the silliest trivial things. They take each other for granted. Maybe they feel like they have years to patch things up. I never felt that way. Not since my mom got sick anyway. I think knowing we didn't have long with her made me value her more. It made all of us value each other more."

"Is that better than her being healthy?" I asked.

"No, I don't think so. But maybe with God's eternal perspective it is."

"Couldn't He teach that lesson in a gentler, kinder way?"

"Probably. But He didn't so I trust there is a reason."

"Why? Why do you trust there is a reason?"

"When there are things I don't know about God, I have to rely on what I *do* know and then proceed from there. I do know that God created the entire universe, and this beautiful planet with you on it! I know that so much of the world is good, and pleasant, and full of beauty. I know the history of God's care and protection of His chosen people, despite terrible enemies and persecution. I know eternity is real and that we are not there yet. It is really no surprise that our temporary home and mortal body would not be quite satisfactory. We are not where we are meant to be yet."

I realized Hank had told me this before, with minor permutations, and stared at him without speaking for a long time. He just returned my gaze, eyebrows raised. He probably wondered if I had developed some sort of catatonic disorder. (By the way, in case you are wondering how I knew the word catatonic, remember I had a drug addict for a father. I can't tell you how many times the medics who revived him called in to the hospital with the description of a "drug overdose in a catatonic patient." Maybe this is an example of a terrible thing being used by God to bring about a good thing…my excellent vocabulary.)

"Do normal Christians speak like this?" I asked finally.

"Am I not a normal Christian?" he asked.

"I don't think so."

"I think every honest Christian has thought about these things," he said, grinning at me.

We might have never returned to working on the aviary door, but Mom appeared on the stoop of the trailer home and called to us.

"Where is Lolita?"

"Dr. Pritchett took her to lunch," I called back.

She scratched her cheek, then cradled her chin, letting that news soak in. Without comment, she turned back and returned indoors.

"Want to learn how to use a circular saw?" Hank asked.

"Sure."

We headed back to the pile of supplies. A banner day. In this single day, I would be broiling my first chicken, cutting my first board with a circular saw, and if Dr. Pritchett had his way, injecting a raptor carcass with healing medicine.

7

You don't need to hear about the broiled chicken. It was not as perfect as I had hoped, but it was edible. I could not really say the same about the baked potato. If you want the details, wait till Hank decides to tell you. I am too ashamed. Let's just say that the good coming out of the bad—we now knew we had a working smoke alarm.

The door to the aviary was successfully completed, mostly without my help. In the nick of time too. The following week, Dr. Pritchett arrived with the two hawks at almost the same time Tim and the Golden Eagle showed up. Tim and Hank raised the two huge floor to roof tarps that would serve as temporary walls till the open hacking tower doors could be closed. I had not seen either Bald Eagle since the brief moment I spied them while rocking on my new deck a couple of days ago. Dr. Pritchett said if they didn't return for a week, he felt we could safely close the doors, lower the far tarp wall, and let the Golden Eagle have a larger flight area as long as another new patient didn't show up who needed the hacking tower.

While our aviary was not as large as a flight cage, it was big enough for the early stages of flight rehab. Tim said it was more than some facilities had to work with.

"You use whatever you have available," he said.

You are probably wondering if after months of caring for my eagles, Tippy and Baldy, I felt any sadness that they seemed to have flown the coop for good. I can honestly say that I felt mostly joy for them. I had successfully helped them return to the big beautiful sky they were supposed to patrol. Only a twinge of selfish sorrow hit me now and then when I glanced at the empty nest.

I liked Tim right away. He was about my mom's age and had similar long grey hair pulled back in a ponytail. He also had an earring in one ear. It was an eagle earring. Because the hawks were still doped up, we decided it would be best to get the Golden Eagle into his enclosure first. Then we would deal with the hawks.

Now I had seen this maneuver before when Baldy was caught and transported to the Florida Raptor Center flight cage for her final weeks of rehab. Eagles are enormous birds, though Golden Eagles are not as large as Bald Eagles. They still have very sharp and dangerous beaks and talons and Tim cautioned us to let only him and Dr. Pritchett handle the eagle.

Mom, Lolita, Mr. Forrest, Hank, and I all lined up along the aviary wall, peering in as Tim and Dr. Pritchett donned heavy long gloves and goggles. Then together they carried the eagle crate into the aviary and carefully shut the new door behind them. The Golden Eagle was not happy about them lifting him out of the crate, but they were quick and in no time had whisked off the protective wraps on his wings, tail, and legs, removed the head cover, and he was released. He spewed a few angry squawks, which I am sure would have gotten his mouth washed out if his mother had been present. I didn't have to speak eagle to know a cussing raptor when I heard one.

Tim and Dr. Pritchett emerged unscathed from the enclosure while the Golden Eagle hopped on the tallest perch and glared at them.

"Well done, Peter!" Lolita said.

Peter? I had never heard anyone call Dr. Pritchett anything but Dr. Pritchett. I guess had I thought about it, I would have known he had a first name, but I sure didn't know what it was till now. What had happened at their lunch together?

He blushed, and shook Tim's hand.

Tim came to me, since I was his official trainee and described what we had done, and asked if I had any questions.

"Why did Goldy have to come here?" I asked.

Hank smiled, overhearing the name of the Golden Eagle. He had told me more than once that my animal's names were on the obvious side.

"He needs some time gaining strength before he is ready for our flight cage. We don't have any room in our aviaries right now. The mid-sized enclosures are bursting with birds. There is even talk of expanding this facility to include a flight cage."

I didn't know that. There wasn't room on my property, that's for sure. Not unless they intended to take over Lightning's pasture. I turned to Mr. Forrest, who must have immediately figured out why I was scowling.

"Across the road," Mr. Forrest told me. "That field is state owned property. We are negotiating with the FWS and seeking government grants, along with private donations. Just starting the process."

"They aren't cheap," Tim said.

"How much are they?" Lolita asked.

"At least $20,000," Tim answered. "If we had one, we'd transfer a couple of our workers here, or train local people. But it's just a pipe dream right at the moment. We aren't close to having funds now."

"So Goldy will go back to Florida Raptor Center for flight training before release?" I asked.

"Yes. And he will probably like that about as much as he liked the five-hour trip over here."

"Well while he's here, along with those new hawks, I'll volunteer and help as much as I can," Lolita said.

"Thank you, ma'am. Speaking of those hawks, Dr. Pritchett…"

Dr. Pritchett nodded and the two men returned to his van, popping open the back doors. The hawks were contained in two separate crates. Mr. Forrest and Hank took one crate, and the other two men took the other. They placed the crates in the enclosure beside Harry's enclosure. Harry watched the proceedings intently. I wondered how he would take to having neighbors.

The two hawks were much more subdued than Goldy. Dr. Pritchett had told me they were not feeling stupendous, with their injuries, surgery, and the aftereffects of the anesthesia. I was surprised they were able to perch, even though it was just a few inches off the floor of the enclosure.

While they were convalescing, I would be chopping up their food and hiding the antibiotics in the mouse pieces. I already had done this for Harry, but Lolita had not had as much practice watching how this was done. I expected her to be squeamish, but she didn't even flinch as Tim showed us what to do.

Goldy was easier to feed. We just tossed a dead fish in his aviary.

"We will need to check on those hawks every few days. A red-shoulder hawk is relatively easy to handle, Leah, and you have watched enough now that with Tim and me here, you can practice learning to grab with the juvenile," Mr. Forrest told me. "And Lolita, the more you watch and help with the other tasks, the sooner you will be able to practice some of the handling."

"Will we start learning to grab with dead birds?" I asked.

Tim grinned. "You've been warned, I see."

I nodded.

"We don't grab the dead birds, except to take them out of the refrigerator. They just don't put up enough of a fight to be of real training value… But I will show you how to put on the anesthesia cap with the dead bird, and how to do some physical therapy like ranging their wings. At first, you'll just watch me do that with the hawks. Goldy won't need any handling, which is good. We try to handle all our patients as little as necessary. It is very stressful for them."

"That's all you need me for today, right Tim?" Dr. Pritchett said.

Lolita glanced his way, and I suspected she wanted to say that was not all she needed from him but she didn't.

Tim agreed Dr. Pritchett and Mr. Forrest were free to get back to their other duties. Dr. Pritchett told Tim he would see him later back at the house. I learned that Tim would be staying with him for the next three weeks while I was being trained and Goldy was convalescing.

Hank had to race off to his construction job, but told me he would drop by the fishing hut after work.

Now Tim had us follow him into our medical shed where Mr. Forrest had already stashed two dead American Kestrels. They were small and easy to work on when dead, he said, but actually difficult when alive.

"Because they are small, it is a delicate balance between grabbing their small parts like those little legs while at the same time not squeezing the body too hard and restricting breathing."

"I guess we don't have to worry about restricting their breathing now," Lolita observed.

"No," Tim agreed.

He spent the afternoon showing us how to restrain them on the anesthesia table, put the cap over their heads where the gas went in, and then how to operate the machine. He didn't actually turn it on, as he didn't want to waste any of the precious resources, but he explained the whole process and then had me repeat the instructions. I messed up a couple of steps, but Lolita surprised me. She remembered everything perfectly. Tim high-fived her, but just told me, "Good job."

Now that our dead birds were anesthetized, he showed us how to slowly stretch out the wings and then refold them. We got to practice that exercise. He told us that would help to keep them limber and prevent scar tissue and adhesions that would negatively affect their flight.

He said sometimes a bird had to receive an injection of medicine, not just oral treatment. He showed us how to fill the syringe, and where to stick the poor bird. We filled it with water and took turns stabbing the carcass. It was fun in a macabre sort of way.

That was all Tim wanted to show us for the day. He re-bagged the dead birds, and put them back in the fridge.

"Did you give them a name?" Lolita asked me.

"Stiff One and Stiff Two," I said. I hope it wasn't callous that we both laughed.

Tim checked on all our birds, and told us he would be back in the morning. Our duties for today were over, except to check on the hawks every hour. If they looked 'worse', call him.

I wasn't certain what 'worse' looked like. Lolita admitted she wasn't certain either. We confessed this after Tim had driven away. So, we sat on the ground outside the hawk enclosure watching them to see if we noticed any difference. They had not moved much. Both remained on the perch they had initially settled on. Both still looked a little hung over from the happy gas. Dr. Pritchett told me it can take quite a while to completely be out of their system, though they had come out of surgery a week ago and were doing fine.

We didn't talk much, but it was not uncomfortable. Mom had disappeared into the trailer after all the birds were settled but now came out and plopped down beside us.

"We need a bench," she said.

It was not the first time one of us had mentioned this. Somehow, we just never got around to building one, or buying some outdoor folding chairs. It occurred to me that Mother's Day was not too far off. Maybe I would get her a chair for Mother's Day. I had never gotten her a Mother's Day gift. This seemed like a good year to start.

"First, I need to dye my hair," Lolita said.

We both swung our heads around to stare at her. That had popped out of the blue.

"Your hair is beautiful," Mom said. "Why do you want to dye it?"

I suspected the blonde was already a dye, but didn't say so. Some people don't go gray, and she probably wasn't quite as old as Mom. She didn't answer. I figured out the answer anyway. She had seen the man in the boat. It had been clear she knew him. She wanted to be as disguised as possible.

She rubbed a long strand between her thumb and forefinger.

"How about purple?" she said.

"That's the rage these days," Mom said, "At least with the Better-Mart crowd."

I wanted to ask her about the man in the boat, but decided not to. If she wasn't comfortable telling us the story that I was certain was painful, I would not force it out of her. I know how people's miserable pasts are sometimes just best left un-raked.

Lightning whinnied, reminding me I had forgotten about her dinner. I'd been so caught up in the new patients that I'd neglected my old friend! Zippy had followed Mom outside, and now yapped his own complaint over his empty stomach.

As I started towards the hay bin, Mom said, "Want to stay for dinner? I'm trying a new recipe."

"Thanks," I said, "But no. I have leftover broiled chicken." As soon as I said that, I thought of the dead carcasses on whom Lolita and I had spent the afternoon practicing our rehab skills. Thoughts of the broiled chicken flipped around in my mind and turned my stomach.

Lightning followed me to the hay bin, as did Zippy. My only regret over the move to the fishing hut was that Lightning wasn't right outside my door anymore. It's true she was only a quarter mile away, but it wasn't the same. I hoped she didn't feel abandoned. Feeling a little guilty, I offered her an extra flake of hay. She nuzzled me, assuring me there was nothing to feel bad about, and dove into her dinner.

"I'll see you in the morning," I said to Mom and Lolita who still sat on the ground, watching the hawks.

They waved and Zippy and I headed down the driveway. Out of habit, I scrutinized the eagle nest, but Tippy and Baldy were not there. I'd hoped at least Tippy would settle in the area, but I hadn't seen any sign of either of them. It would be no surprise that Baldy would return to the old nest where she and her mate lived before she was shot out of the sky. That's what the rehab expert thought she would do.

Young eagles do not remain with their parents and usually fly off to new hunting grounds. I shouldn't complain. Even if Tippy was gone for good, all kinds of new life was starting around here. Hank and I were getting married…soon. Lolita was starting a new career and leaving whatever nasty memories of her former life she had behind her. Hank told me he had applied for the Wildlife Officer program, which would mean he'd have to commute back and forth from Florida Gateway college at times.

A flight cage was being considered for our Kumsquat Raptor Center! No, I had plenty of new excitement ahead of me.

With Zippy right on my heel, I arrived at the fishing hut. Instead of rushing inside, I plopped down on my white rocking chair on the deck and heaved a deep sigh, considering a disturbing fact. I tended to attract creatures that were what some folks would call bottom-feeders. Not only were the animals who had flocked to me damaged in various ways, but my new career as a raptor rehabilitator was all about broken and injured wildlife. And now Lolita.

I must give off some sort of scent.

Except for Hank. He was not a misfit. He was the most perfect human being ever created. Not that I have met all of God's creation, but I have met most of the scumbags and Hank doesn't share a single molecule of likeness to them. Believe me. I know.

Speaking of perfection, Hank appeared right then and settled down beside me. He smelled like the outdoors and sweat. Honest sweat. Not the sweat I remembered oozing out of my parent's armpits when there was a knock on the door accompanied by the words: "Police. Open up."

"How was training on dead birds?" he asked.

"Fine. Can we order pizza?"

He smiled. He remembered the broiled chicken too.

"Sure. It is a celebration. I have some amazing news."

"In the last three hours since I last saw you?"

"Just in the last hour. Dad just called. An anonymous donor donated $20,000 for a new Kumsquat Raptor Center Flight Cage."

"*What?* Seriously?"

"Seriously. With the small grants Dad was able to scrounge up, that is enough to break ground immediately. He is almost certain we can lease the land just across the road from your trailer. For now. Ultimately, we would purchase it, but since it is a non-profit organization, the cost will be minimal."

"Who would do that? Who would even *know* about the need?"

Hank shrugged. "The Florida Raptor Center knows the donor, but the deal is off if the donor is revealed."

"Wow."

I shook my head. In my world, things like this just did not happen. Not until I met Hank.

"Of course, God knew about the need," Hank said.

That was expected. Hank always gave God the credit. Since I was brand new to this whole God-thing, I was not at all in the habit of going to God as the source of all good things happening. Until I met Hank really nothing much good happened, to be honest.

"Do you think God is the anonymous donor?" I asked.

"I think maybe God prompted the anonymous donor."

"How?"

This may seem like a stupid question for anyone who has been walking with God for more than a few weeks like me. However, I was deadly serious. How does God prompt anyone to do anything?

"Through the Holy Spirit," Hank answered immediately.

"What's that?" It sounded spooky, whatever it was.

"When anyone trusts Jesus as Lord, the Holy Spirit enters that person. The Bible talks about the Holy Spirit as a helper, a guide, and a friend that will convict us of right and wrong and help us to hear and follow God."

"Well I trusted Jesus as Lord."

"Yes."

Hank had been there. He had heard me pray to ask Jesus into my life, to tell Him I believed He was who He said He was, crazy as the whole story sounded. I did believe it too. I don't know why exactly, but I did.

"So then why haven't I heard the Holy Spirit prompt *me*?"

"Maybe you have, but you didn't know it was the Holy Spirit."

"Like when?"

"Well, how about when Lolita crashed on our shore. And you offered her, a complete stranger who we are pretty sure was not in a legal career, your home?"

I considered this. That actually was a little out of character for me. I did not, generally speaking, trust strangers. Especially not strangers who were almost certainly prostitutes running from the law in a stolen boat.

"Would the Holy Spirit have prompted me to hide a criminal?" I asked.

Hank looked deeply into my eyes, pondering.

"That is a very good question," he said, after a long pause.

"Do you have a very good answer?"

"No. I don't think the Holy Spirit would ever prompt us to sin. He is to guide us in all righteousness, the Bible says. Harboring a criminal knowingly would be sin. So if the Holy Spirit prompted you, then she is not a criminal as far as you know."

"But I sure think she is. I think she probably stole the boat, don't you?"

"That reminds me…I need to try to fix that boat. But yes…I did at first. I am not so sure now."

"And I am also pretty sure she is a hooker. Aren't you?" Here Hank paused.

"I think maybe she is, but not of her own choice."

"What do you mean? She is my mother's age. It's not like she's a kid being forced into sexual slavery."

"No…but we don't know the whole story. She is afraid. We know that. And I don't sense evil in her. I did sense evil in the man in the boat."

I agreed with Hank on all that. I wondered if that was the Holy Spirit talking.

"How can we help her if we don't know her story?" I asked.

"I don't know. I think she needs to know she can trust us…and maybe she will tell you her story."

Or maybe she would tell Peter Pritchett.

8

The next time I was alone with Lolita was while we were dicing dead mice and hiding antibiotics inside the gross little pieces. (The train-wreck hawks got hidden pain-killers as well.) Not the most conducive setting in which to pry deep hidden secrets, but you work with what you are given.

And just so you know, Lolita was now a brunette.

"Your mom helped," Lolita told me. "What do you think?"

I think you are hiding, and I want to know why.

I didn't say *that* out loud. "Nice."

She could hide her blondness, but she couldn't hide her gorgeousness. I wondered if she had considered that. While I was searching for some sort of an opening to ask her if she sold her body for profit and if the man chasing her was one of her clients she had stolen a boat from, she said, "I appreciate you haven't nosed around in my business."

I closed my mouth on the nosing-in-her-business words that were on the verge of tumbling from my tongue.

"I know how this must look to you."

She pushed the new brunette locks off her face, flipping them behind her shoulder. I scraped the mouse morsels into three separate bowls. I couldn't come up with anything to say that wouldn't be insulting so I kept my lips zipped.

"When I was fifteen, I ran away from home. I told you my dad abused me, pretty much anyway you can imagine, and I finally decided I'd had enough. But I had no place to go, no money, no one who would help me. I ended up on the streets, hiding out as best I could.

"Unfortunately, I was desperate, and it was heading into winter. A creep who patrolled the hiding places of girls like me gathered us up, and gave us food, clothes, shelter, and a job."

She paused here. I didn't have to expend too much brain activity deciphering what her job was.

"Did you try to escape?" I asked.

She looked down, and shook her head. "To what? I was a kid, and one that had been bludgeoned into believing I was worthless and damaged goods. We had a warm place to stay and we didn't go hungry. Eventually, I was the favorite girl of one of the wealthier men. I was not stupid, and I managed to convince him to put me up in my own apartment, and be his personal 'escort' when he was in town. That lasted a couple of years. Then I got pregnant. He threatened to kill me if I didn't abort that baby. He promised to take care of me, just like he had been up to that point, if I aborted. So I did. Three times. Then, when I was pregnant with the fourth baby, I ran again. I took all the trinkets he had bought me, and the fancy clothes, and pawned them. That gave me enough for a bus ticket to Miami. On the way, I miscarried. All those abortions…they mess with your body."

I had stopped dicing mice, and was staring at her with my mouth hanging open. Fortunately, she was eyeing the bowls of hawk food, and didn't notice. By the time she glanced up, I had snapped my jaw shut.

"Gross," she said.

"We won't have to cut them up for much longer. Starting tomorrow we give Harry a whole mouse. He will be done with the antibiotics."

"Not the mice…though they are pretty gross. My story. The abortions, the life…"

I know my eyes were wide and I looked like a mannequin frozen in mid pose at a horror movie, but I was struggling to find anything hopeful to say in the wake of this dismal tale. I thought *I* had a lousy life. My life was Buckingham Palace compared to Lolita's.

For whatever reason, maybe the need to unburden herself of all those wretched memories, Lolita continued with her story.

"So in Miami, I went back to doing the only thing I knew how to do. I won't burn your ears out with the details, but I ended up working as a high-end escort. The money was pretty incredible, but it took me a few years to work up to that level. I had put away a good bit of money and was thinking of retiring. That was when I met the owner of the boat that keeps going by, that man you saw. He's a cop."

Now that was a twist I hadn't expected.

"You can stuff your eyes back in their sockets Don't look so shocked! I didn't do anything wrong. I mean nothing any more wrong than the escort business. The cop fell for me. Hard. I didn't come cheap, and I figured he was doing some dirty deals on the side to be able to afford me. I didn't know he was a cop, of course. Not at first. I would never have been with him. Last thing I needed was to be busted.

"I found out he was a cop by accident. Saw him on the news in a drug bust. I knew I had to run, fast. I assumed he was investigating prostitution rings in Miami. The cops usually leave the high-end escort business alone, but there are plenty of undercover agents trying to bust the sex traffic rings. Then, I started snooping around when he'd be passed out after… well… Anyway, I found ledgers, stuffed in a drawer, filled with girls' names, men's names, and dollar amounts paid. Sure looked like he was a John, running his own little prostitution ring. I took pictures with my phone… just in case he ever tried to bust me. I'd have proof he was a dirty cop. Something happened. I don't want to talk about that. But I knew I had to leave, right away. I had enough money. I didn't need to do this life anymore.

"I moved to the Gulf area, and thought I had it made. That life behind me, enough money in the bank to last me forever. Changed my name. New life." Here Lolita let out a string of obscenities. "Then he found me, nearly ten years later. Visiting the Gulf area. Ran into me in a coffee shop. Wondered why I had just disappeared without a trace. I got out of there, but then he showed up on the doorstep of my apartment. I don't know how he tracked me down, but he threatened to arrest me for prostitution. I don't even know if he could do that since I was retired…but I was scared. I played along. I didn't know what to do, honestly. I didn't want to go to jail. I was afraid if I ran, he would either kill me or arrest me. Who would take my word over a cop?

"I went back to his hotel, thinking I'd tell him about my pictures that would have him hauled off to jail. I didn't quite know how to do it without endangering me. He didn't let me out of his sight that week, but I learned a pretty useful fact. He was in the Gulf collecting girls for his sex ring.

"It wasn't hard to figure out with a little snooping. He busted them for drugs, and then told them he wouldn't arrest them if they would work for him. The idiot… had the names of them and pictures of them with the drugs. I have no idea if that would be enough to convict them but these were young, doped up runaways. Scared.…I bided my time, and when he would get high or drunk, passed out, I started collecting photographs of evidence of what he was doing. I was no angel, but the thought of what he was doing with those girls…given my background…"

Here she paused and covered her face.

I didn't have to ask why she hadn't escaped that week. I knew what guilt, fear, and shame could do to a psyche. If you haven't lived it, it's hard to understand.

"What were you going to do with your evidence?" I asked, finally when she didn't continue with her story, her face still hidden by her fingers stretched out like a protective net to catch all the grief.

"Report him, eventually. But, like I said, I didn't know how to do that without incriminating myself. I had plenty of evidence by now. Some of the girls sometimes showed up to his hotel room while I was there. He'd collect the money, and give them their 'cut.' I even got pictures of that. That turned out to be my undoing."

"What happened?"

"One of the girls came and went…he never let them in. He didn't know I even saw them. He conducted that business in the hallway. But he saw that I was standing near the hallway when he closed the door. I stumbled, and didn't back off in time, and I think he knew I'd seen the girl. I joked, asked if I wasn't enough for him. We had the television on and there was a picture of that same girl…it was a news report about missing teens in the Gulf area. I knew enough to pretend I hadn't seen it, but I also know he suspected I had. He turned the TV off right away."

She stood and moved to the door of the little medical shed, looking out at the river.

"Is that his boat?" I asked.

"No. I had one friend in the Gulf area. First platonic relationship with a man I'd ever had. Great guy. Lost a wife to cancer. I met him at a park when I first moved to the Gulf. We became friends. He knew some of my story. I knew his. He'd take me on his boat sometimes. He was mourning his wife. He just needed a friend to talk to …and Lord knows *I* did.

"I left the cop's place, terrified. Told him I was going to the bathroom, and climbed out the window. I didn't know what he would do to me if he found out I had all those photos on my phone that proved he was running a prostitution ring with runaway teens. I was sure when I walked out of the bathroom, he would shoot me. He knew I'd seen the girl and he knew I wasn't stupid. I could see in his face that the jig was up.

"Anyway, I was afraid to go home but I went anyway and gathered my bank cards and a few bits of clothes. I figured I needed to get out of there fast. I thought of my friend, Greg. I hadn't seen Greg for years, but I went directly there. That's why I was wearing the clothes you saw me in. I never wore that kind of get up. The cop liked it…but I didn't want to take the time to change."

"Greg lived along the river, not too far from me. I got a cab, went to Greg's, a crying mess, and told him the story. He wanted me to go to the police. I didn't know who to trust in the police department, and I was afraid I'd be arrested. Greg gave me the keys to his boat, told me to find a safe place, and send the evidence from my phone to the cops. He knew if I tried to escape in my car, the cop would put an APB on the tags."

This was as unbelievable a story as I had ever heard.

"Did you do that?" I asked. "Did you send your evidence to the police?"

"No. He'll kill me."

"Not if he's in jail. How did he know to look for you on the river?"

"I don't know."

"Did he know about your friend, Greg?"

"I don't know that either. He is a detective. I imagine he pieced together some stuff."

"My friend is an honest cop," I told her. "You would be safe telling him your story."

She shook her head. "I don't want to go to jail."

I had no idea if she could go to jail for her years of prostitution. "Maybe I could find out without giving you away," I said. "You'd be helping those girls."

Her eyes filled with tears.

"Is there a chance he knows you have those pictures?"

She nodded. "He's looking for me. He must suspect. He knows I escaped out his bathroom window. He probably figures I had a good reason, other than the fact that he's a filthy, low-down pig."

The hawks screeched, reminding us we had not delivered their breakfast yet. I handed Lolita Harry's dish and I took the other two. I watched as Lolita opened the little feeding hatch to Harry's cage and attached the bowl to the holder. Harry waited for the door to close and then moved quickly to gobble down his food.

The two hawks that had collided with the train looked a little perkier than they had last night. They remained perched on the two lowest perches. I wondered if they had moved at all. I put the bowls in the front lower section of their cage and backed away. They hopped off the perch and wobbled a little clumsily to the food, the juvenile first, followed by Mama.

"Peter told me if they ate this morning, he was confident they would recover. He said they were really lucky."

Lucky? Flying into a train? I was still wondering how Lolita had managed to get on a first name basis in one meal when I had not even heard Mr. Forrest call him anything but Dr. Pritchett, and they were old friends.

"He said it could have been a whole lot worse."

Lightning nickered, hearing our voices, and trotted to the fence edge. That startled Goldy who flew to a higher perch across the aviary. My eyes traveled up the live oak at the edge of the hacking tower where the eagle nest remained empty.

Both of us went to Lightning and received sweet nuzzles in return. "That's her way of saying bring on the chow," I said.

Once Lightning was munching away on her grain and hay, I showed Lolita where the fish for Goldy was stashed in the refrigerator. I didn't even walk in the enclosure. Just tossed it onto the grass near his perch.

"That's it for now," I said. "Dr. P wants us to be sure all of them are eating. If not, we have to force feed them and he said that is not fun. They were eating before he brought them here so he's not super worried. So your friend…Greg…Does he want his boat back?"

Lolita cast a quick look at the boat. "Probably. I've been afraid to call. I mean the cop is a detective. He could trace my calls if he wanted to, right?"

I shrugged. "You can use my phone."

Mom blasted out of the trailer now, waving to us both.

"I'm late!" she called as she scurried to the VW. "Lolita, help yourself to whatever you want. I'll be back around 4!"

She squealed out of the driveway and left in a wake of dust.

Tim and Dr. Pritchett arrived just as the dust from Mom's car was settling.

"Time for PT!" Tim said, hopping out of the car. Goldy had to be encouraged to fly or he would stiffen up. So Tim showed me how to walk towards the eagle who would fly to a different corner of the aviary in response. He didn't have access to the tree yet, but Dr. Pritchett told me if the eagles didn't return in two more nights, we could close the tower doors and open the full back half of the aviary to Goldy.

"But we'll slide the tarp wall over and have an area sectioned off for Harry. He needs a bigger flight space."

"Can all three of the hawks share the same area?" I asked.

He was about to answer, but the dolphins materialized just off shore and they were raising a ruckus. They were very agitated, all of them surfacing, clicking, whistling and smacking their tails down on the water. I had never seen all of them so explosive before.

"Hide," I said to Lolita. She didn't question me, but instantly ducked into the Medical shed. Just in time. The scowling man that I now knew was the cop who was hunting for her appeared yet again in his motorboat, skidding across the water and around the bend. He zoomed right by us, so I wondered if we were no longer on his suspect list. There was no doubt the dolphins had appeared to warn us. You can laugh if you want, but the facts speak for themselves. Had the dolphins not appeared and been so upset, I would not have warned Lolita, and the dirty cop would have seen her.

I stole a look at Dr. P who was perplexed. He had heard me tell Lolita to hide. If he didn't know her situation, he was probably wondering about it now. I went to the shed and pushed open the door.

"He's gone," I whispered.

"Was it him?"

I nodded.

She shook her head and slumped onto a metal stool.

"He didn't even slow down," I said, "I don't think he is looking for you here anymore."

"Maybe not, but he's still looking."

"Who's looking for you?" Dr. Pritchett asked. He stood behind me, peering at the trembling Lolita.

Lolita sighed and pursed her lips. "A terrible man. He won't take no for an answer."

Tim poked his head around Dr. P.

"I'd like to evaluate how mobile the red-tail hawk is."

"Harry?" I asked.

Tim smiled. "Ok, Harry. The one in the end cage."

"His bandage just came off yesterday," Dr. P said. "Range is unrestricted. He hasn't been flying much. Just up to the perch."

We all looked up at the eagle's nest now. I knew what was needed. If they closed the aviary tower doors, Goldy could be moved to the larger enclosure with the nest and tree, and Harry could have the middle section.

Dr. P looked at me probably to gauge whether I was going to collapse in a puddle of self-pity over my eagles.

"I was hoping they would stay for the wedding," I said, "But it looks like they had other plans."

"They haven't been back for several nights," Dr. P explained to Tim.

"Are we good with closing those doors?" he asked.

Dr. P looked at me. I nodded.

"The aviary is a good size if can open the whole length…but we can't have the eagles and hawks together."

"Dan is getting a final decision today he thinks on the land lease across the street."

"Any idea who is funding the flight cage?" Dr. P asked Tim.

Tim shook his head. "All I was told is that if the donor is revealed the deal is off."

"Hmmmm. Not many folks would be so generous and humble."

"No," Tim agreed.

Lolita kept swiveling her head to look at the river. I was not alone in straining to hear any sounds of a returning motor boat.

"Well, we could have it built in a month with the Florida Raptor crew," Tim said. "That's close to the time we need it for the Golden Eagle. It would make this facility a whole lot more useful."

"We'll close those doors and open the tarp enough to scare Goldy into that portion," Tim said. "Then we can relocate Harry to this middle section. He will need to start exercising his wings, Leah. We start watching how he flies the cage length, and if he looks all right, we start with maybe 6-8 lengths. You will need to keep daily notes for me on how he handles that. We look for his stamina, how well he glides, whether he is smooth using the affected wing. His general coordination."

"When does he graduate to whole mice?" Lolita asked, wrenching her attention off the river.

"Not soon enough for you I bet," Tim said.

Dr. P smiled. "Harry is done with the antibiotics, so he can have whole mice now. The train wreck pair will need another two weeks for meds. With their leg injury, we better continue with cut up food so they don't stress the fracture site."

"Do they graduate to live mice at some point?" I asked. Lolita shuddered. Funny that she would find live mice scarier than chopping off their little heads and limbs. (If that disgusts you even to *read* the words, I would strongly suggest you not consider a career in raptor rehab.)

"We evaluate that by how well and how quickly they recover flight. Hard to catch a mouse otherwise."

"I can help you with the aviary doors," Dr. P said to Tim.

Now that they weren't watching me for mental collapse, I have to say I felt a wave of grief as they closed the doors blocking the nest from my eagles. Lolita patted my shoulder.

"I know what it feels like to have to say goodbye to a child," she said.

I thought that was an odd thing to say. She had not mentioned any children. Just three abortions in her sad story this morning. I was also touched by her unexpected empathy for my sadness over the baby eagle I had raised leaving the nest for good.

Maybe my face registered confusion because she quickly amended her statement, "I mean I can imagine how it must feel."

"He was a good eagle baby," I said, sniffling.

I was indeed a little weepy, but I was eyeing Lolita. She was hiding something. What child had she said goodbye to? Why did she leave that out of her story?

9

Hank arrived around dinner time. I asked if he would stay for leftover broiled chicken and pizza. He said that sounded wonderful.

"Oh…I probably should add a vegetable…there's onions and peppers on the pizza."

"That works," Hank said.

I did not deserve Hank. I made a mental note to buy green things from the grocery store tomorrow.

"We closed the aviary doors today," I told him.

"Oh Leah. I'm sorry. I know that was not easy for you."

"No. But Goldy was thrilled. Tim spooked him into the tree half of the aviary and he flew up into the tree right away."

"How did he look?"

"A little lopsided while he was flying. Tim said it wasn't bad for the longest flight he's done so far since his wing was broken. Hank…how long after being a prostitute can someone be arrested for it?"

Hank raised an eyebrow.

"Is there something you want to tell me?"

I smiled. "It's about Lolita…"

"I think there has to be proof of that person engaging in prostitution or no charges can be filed."

Now that was encouraging! I knew Lolita was only paid in cash, and did no advertising. Her clients were through word of mouth.

Then I relayed Lolita's story and her last statement about knowing how hard it is to say goodbye to a child.

"Maybe she meant the aborted babies. It didn't sound like she wanted the abortions. Or the miscarriage."

"Maybe, but somehow, I don't think so. I felt like she was hiding something."

"It's hard to believe she would share that she was abused, forced into prostitution, then became a high-end hooker and is running away from a dirty cop intending to expose him for running a sex trafficking ring using runaway drug addicts…and would still be hiding something."

"Well, when you put it like that… I asked her to let us talk to William. Show him the evidence on her phone. She said no. She's afraid she will be arrested."

"Hmmm. I don't know. Prostitution *is* illegal."

"But she's not a prostitute now."

"We'd have to talk to a lawyer probably…or William."

"Hank…that cop went by on his boat again. He didn't slow down this time by our place, but he is still out looking. Do you think we are in danger?"

"It's possible," he said. "I stopped by there on my way over. She dyed her hair. I didn't recognize her from a distance."

"If she *could* be arrested…well…what would God have us do? Turn her in?"

Hank sighed and shook his head slowly.

"She's not a prostitute now. Let me see what I can find out. I won't involve William or share any names. Dad knows lots of guys in law enforcement."

I dished out our leftovers and we took our plates out to the deck. It was not too hot in the shade of the deck, with the roof blocking the sun. We balanced the plates on our laps and I tried not to picture the dead Kestrels as I cut into my broiled chicken.

"I talked with Pastor Rimerton."

I munched on the wad of chicken.

"He is available in four Saturdays to do a wedding."

"Ours?" I asked.

"I know that's rushing…but if you think you could have your dress by then. Really since we are having it on our property, I thought maybe we could just cater a dinner afterwards right there. Not many people will be invited. What do you think?"

"I think I better learn how to make a second dinner so you won't totally regret marrying me."

He smiled. "Is that yes?"

"The sooner the better," I said. "Do I *have* to wear a wedding dress?"

"How about if you and I take a trip to Orlando? While Tim is here he can work with Lolita and my dad to take care of the hawks. We can do a day trip, be back by night. Get the rings, and a dress."

"I would like that," I said. Frankly I surprised myself. I don't know why Hank had decided to hurry wedding plans along, but I was glad. "And will that be all right with your parents?"

"They know about Lolita and the strange man looking for her. They would just as soon you not be alone as soon as possible."

"I'm not alone," I told him. His face lit up and I think maybe he thought I was about to tell him God was with me. That is not what I was about to say, and only thought of it at all because I know that is how he thinks. I would have lied, just to make him happy, but decided in my new life as a Christian, that would not be right either.

"I mean Zippy is here."

Hank nodded. "That's true. And Zippy helped catch the eagle poacher."

"I'll be ok," I said, putting my plate on the deck floor so the ever-present Zippy could snap up any leftover atoms of food. "I have my gun."

I *did* have a gun too. I had never used it, but I knew how to fire it. William, my cop friend, had taught me when the eagle poacher was on the loose and everyone was worried I was in danger. It turns out they were right.

"Keep it near you at night," Hank said. "I don't like the story about that dirty cop."

"He's not interested in me," I said.

"He would be if he knew Lolita told you her story."

"If the story is true…and I believe she is telling me the truth, would the police be able to use her proof to bust that dirty cop?"

"I don't know, Leah. It seems to me they would, but I haven't seen her proof. It can't be too hard to find out how long the statute of limitations is in Florida for an ex-prostitute. Let's google it."

I went into the hut and grabbed my laptop. When I came back out, Flash had arrived under our dock. None of the rest of his pod appeared to be with him. He was fishing in the shade of the dock. I leaned over the railing and called to him.

Instantly he lifted his head and emitted a series of clicks. I clicked back, which seemed to satisfy whatever conversational needs he had, and he dipped back underwater.

"I wish I knew what we just said to each other," I said, sighing.

Hank was already scrolling through some hits on his search for statute of limitations.

"Ah ha!" Hank said. "Look."

I read the paragraph he was pointing at. The federal statute of limitations for solicitation and prostitution was one year.

"And look here. In Florida, prostitution is a 3rd degree felony. The statute of limitations is 3 years for that. She's been retired longer than that."

"Then Lolita is safe," I said. "She can report the cop."

"As long as she can prove she was being held against her will by that dirty cop before she escaped. She was not dressed like someone retired from prostitution when we met her," Hank said.

"I'll talk to her tomorrow."

Which I intended to do, but Tim was already there, eager to be exercising Harry when I arrived back at the aviary in the morning. He also wanted to go over the treatment plan of the two new patients and the morning had slipped away by the time he was finished. Lolita was with us for the training. She was as enthusiastic as always, until her phone buzzed. She glanced at a text message, and became immediately subdued and distracted. Tim led me into the far enclosure to show me how to entice Harry to fly from side to side of the aviary. When we finished, Lolita was nowhere to be found.

I had no idea where she had gone.

I spent the day hanging out by the water with my animal friends in between checking on the recuperating hawks, and she had still not materialized. I hoped she hadn't run away again. Mom was at work with the rust-mobile, so if Lolita had run off, it was by foot.

Mom showed up while I was tossing Lightning her dinner.

"Hi," I said, "Do you know where Lolita is?"

"She's not here?" Mom asked.

"No, she slipped out without me even noticing this morning. I haven't seen her since."

Mom's brow wrinkled in concern. I followed Mom into the trailer with the same dismal thought. What had she taken? Strangely, she had not taken her suitcase, nor any of the few things that could be considered remotely valuable in our house. Like the toaster. Nothing was out of place. Except Lolita.

"That man that she was afraid of…he didn't come by, did he?"

"Not that I saw," I said. "She got a text that seemed to bother her."

"Was it from him?"

"I don't know. She was gone before I could ask."

Mom plopped down on the couch. "She is definitely bothered about something. Last night she had a screaming nightmare. I couldn't tell what she was screaming, except one word: Melanie."

"Who is Melanie?"

Mom shrugged. "Maybe that's her real name."

I looked around the living room, thinking maybe there was some sort of clue of where she had gone. We heard a car crunching down our driveway then, and looked out to see Dr. Pritchett arriving. Guess who was in the front seat?

Lolita hopped out. Then she leaned into the car, pulled something out of her purse and handed it to Dr. P. It caught the sun. Something metallic.

Dr. Pritchett waved to us as he backed out.

"We were worried about you," Mom said instantly when Lolita reached us.

Lolita looked surprised. "Why?"

"You were gone all day and we didn't know where. With that man you are so afraid of looking for you…we just didn't want you to be in any danger."

Lolita looked like she was about to cry. "Thank you for caring. I had errands to run, and didn't want to bother you. Peter saw me walking back from the post office and gave me a lift. It turned out to be a further walk than I expected."

"Is everything Ok?" Mom asked.

"Fine," she said. But I didn't think her face looked fine at all. I think she looked scared. And for the life of me, I could not imagine what errands she could be running in the decrepit town of Kumsquat.

"I can help with the dinners for the hawks," she said to me.

I nodded, and she followed me to the aviary. I was itching to talk with her about the dirty cop, but had no idea how to broach the subject delicately. Finally, I decided to just let it spew.

"That dirty cop…did he text you today?"

Lolita startled, and her eyes darted around the grounds, as though he were lurking nearby. "No."

"You looked upset," I said.

She didn't answer. She pulled open the refrigerator door in the medical shed and found the packages of diced mice. We spent the next few minutes measuring the antibiotics into the mouse bits.

"I don't mean to pry," I finally said in the yawning silence, "But I found out something that might ease your mind."

Her hands were shaking as she spooned the proper weight of mice into the new hawk patients' bowls.

"According to Florida law, you can't be prosecuted for…your past work. Not anymore. Not after three years."

She looked up, her mouth dropping open. "Are you sure?"

"Hank and I checked it at a few different government sites. That cop can't have you arrested. We think you need to go to the police with the evidence you have."

"I can't. Not yet. He'll kill me before he'd let me testify against him."

"Do you have those photos, those ledgers you told me about, copied somewhere safe?"

She nodded. "I do now."

Oh. Now I knew what errands. She'd run to the post office.

"Then you are safe."

"You don't understand everything," she said.

"Then tell William…my friend who is a policeman. You can trust him. He will help you."

"There is…someone else…in danger. Not just me. I can't. Not yet."

I shook my head. I couldn't imagine what she was talking about.

"Leah, I appreciate what all of you are doing. I will go to your friend. Soon. Just not yet. I have to think it all through."

Her features looked so brittle that I thought if I touched her she would shatter into tiny pieces. Maybe Hank would be able to help me figure out what she could possibly be waiting for.

"Is the evidence copied. In a safe deposit box?"

She nodded. "Peter has the key."

We gathered the bowls of food, including a whole mouse for Harry. Tim said that we would start feeding Harry live mice tomorrow. We'd supplement with dead ones if he was unsuccessful catching them. I told Lolita that news as I tossed the dead mouse into Harry's enclosure.

She smiled, but just barely.

It was a pretty hot day for being so early in the spring. We finished feeding everyone, and wandered to the river to dip our feet in the cool water. Zippy tagged along on our heels, then pounced on minnows in the shallow pools among the reeds.

"Why are you helping me?" she asked.

I thought for a moment. I wasn't positive I knew the answer to that, so I said the first thing that popped in my head. I must've been channeling Hank, because it was much more a Hank-like statement than something I would come up with.

"I think that's what God wants me to do."

"God wants you to help a hooker running from the law?"

"Well, maybe not exactly *that*…but I think He would want me to help someone who had no one else to turn to. I mean… a couple of years ago that was me."

"No one helped *you*," she said.

"That's not true. Hank helped me. And so did my animals. And honestly…." Here I paused because I had never really admitted what I was about to say to anyone. In fact, I hadn't really realized it till right then and there. "So did God."

"How did God help you?"

"I was all alone. Or I thought I was. I didn't see any good reason to trust anyone…or to forgive anyone either. The last thing I wanted in my life was my mother. God sent me Lightning, and then my job, and then a bicycle. And I crashed my bicycle and He sent me a Bible right there on the road. And then Hank. And Hank talked to me in a way that made me want to read that Bible. And that started me thinking about God and how much He loved me…I don't know. It all came together that He was there. And He was real. And I wasn't alone. Just knowing that gave me the strength to do what I needed to do. And he gave me a second chance at a family. I never thought I'd want my mother in my life again…but you know…I'm glad she's there now. Most of the time, anyway. I didn't think I'd ever feel that way."

"God used up all His good miracles on you," Lolita said. "And I don't blame Him. You are a sweet girl, Leah. They would be wasted on me. There's a few too many decades of sin to wash away."

"That's not what the Bible says."

She smiled at me, but there was a pool of sadness in her eyes.

"In fact, did you know that one of Jesus' ancestors was a prostitute?" I was pretty impressed with myself that I knew this, but I had finally slogged my way through some of the rough boring books of the Bible like Leviticus and Numbers and had reached the book of Joshua. I had just read the pretty astounding chapter 2 of Joshua and even talked with Hank about it because I didn't understand. Now I explained to Lolita.

"When Joshua, the leader of Israel sent spies into Jericho to see if they could take the city by force, they hid in the home of Rahab, a prostitute."

Lolita's eyes popped open at that.

"Bet they didn't tell their wives," she said.

"They didn't stay with her for *that*," I said. "At least, maybe not. It was probably a good place to hide, since travelers going to a prostitute wouldn't arouse much interest. I guess traveling men going to a prostitute would be…common."

"Uh…*yeah*," Lolita agreed.

"But these spies were men of God, and Rahab later hides them from her own people, and even says she knows that the spies worshiped the one true God. I don't know how she knew that. My guess is they were different from other men she knew. Maybe they told her about God. At any rate, she saved the spies from being found and killed by soldiers who were looking for them. The spies escaped, and the Israelites successfully attacked and took Jericho. Rahab wasn't killed though. And she ended up marrying one of the spies, who became the father of Boaz, and is listed in the genealogy of Jesus Himself."

"Well, well," Lolita said.

"I don't know as much about the Bible as Hank does," I told her, "But I do know this. I was a pretty wretched messed up piece of work, and God changed me. And my mother was worse. And God changed her. If He can do that to us, He can do that to anyone."

"Why would He want to?" she asked. "I mean with all the good people around, why would He bother with garbage like me?"

"I don't think He makes garbage. The Bible says all of us are made in His image."

Now, I was no expert in scripture, that goes without saying. However, that particular line I remembered because it was another passage I asked Hank about. I wanted to know exactly which one of our images most closely resembled God. It doesn't take a genius to figure out that our images are all different, unless we are identical twins. Which most of us are not.

Hank told me that His image is not flesh and blood, since the Bible says God is spirit. Image refers to immaterial things like intellect, ability to reason, consciousness, and moral code. Hank said nothing else in all creation reflects God that way other than humans. It is what gives us our value. I felt pretty special after that discussion.

"And besides that," I said, "The Bible also says that there are none that are good but God alone. We all sin and don't have any chance of making it to heaven by being good enough."

"Well now that's something we can agree on," Lolita said.

I bet she had seen her share of depraved people in her line of work.

"In fact," Lolita said, "It seems kind of cruel of God to dangle Heaven in our face and then tell us we are all too despicable to go there."

"Well I didn't say we can't go there," I said. "We *can* but not by our own goodness, cause like you noticed, none of us are good enough."

"How do we get there?" she asked.

If you want to know the truth, at this point, I wanted to tell her to ask Hank. I know I believed the Bible, but I felt a little like an imbecile explaining it to anyone else. Frankly, it is a crazy story. How do you tell someone with a straight face that you believe that God came to earth as a human being, committed no sin, convinced us to understand that we were steeped in sin basically from the moment we learned how to say NO, that God required a penalty for sin, that Jesus agreed freely to pay that penalty for us, and all we had to do was be honestly sorry for our sin, and tell Jesus we accepted His offer and believed He could save us from our wretched lives of sin so that we could go to Heaven? How could I say that to her? To anyone?

So at first, I clammed up. I glanced down the driveway and prayed that Hank would miraculously appear. Even Mom would probably do a better job at this than I would. I even hoped the dolphins might show up and start chattering to distract her from expecting an answer.

But here's the strangest thing. She wasn't mocking me anymore. She wanted to know. She asked again!

"How do we get to heaven if we can't get there by earning our way?"

I looked around, with a touch of franticness, but there was no one else. So I told her. I sounded ridiculous, even to myself, but I soldiered on and did my best. I for sure could not remember any specific verses, but I told her my story and how Hank explained it all to me.

When I finished, I shrugged, and sputtered to a stop. I'd been looking out at the water while I talked, hoping beyond hope for Flash and Pinky to start leaping into the air so all the attention wasn't on me. Now I took a deep breath, and looked at Lolita.

Tears were streaming down her cheeks. Big mascara tinged rivulets of sorrow.

"I want to believe that," she said.

"Well, I think that's probably the first step," I said hopefully.

10

Hank and I decided that Saturday was the perfect time to go dress and ring shopping. He told me we would get a diamond engagement ring right away and he was sorry we hadn't done that already. I told him all I wanted was a simple gold wedding band. I had never cared about jewelry and I was certain I would snag any diamond on horse tails or dog fur, or hay bales.

"Do you mind?" I asked.

He laughed. "Well, if you insist, I won't spend $5,000 on a diamond ring."

I gasped. "Is that really what they cost??"

"The cheaper ones."

Now that's sick, if you ask me.

Tim assured us that between him, Lolita, and Mom, the hawks would be well cared for and we could go have a fine day in Orlando.

"And the dress…" I said.

"What about it?" Hank asked.

"Do I have to get a real wedding dress?"

Hank grinned at me. "What do you mean by a real wedding dress?"

"All frou-frou with lace and beads and pearl buttons. I don't think I could wear something like that."

"You don't have to get anything you don't want to get," Hank said.

"Would it bother you if I walked down the aisle in my shorts and t-shirt?"

He paused here. Finally, he took a deep breath and said, "Yes."

I sighed.

"But you don't need a frou-frou dress with lace and beads and pearl buttons. Maybe you could get a simpler white dress."

"I think I could do that," I said.

"Though it is your one legitimate day to dress like a princess," Hank said. "Are you sure you want to pass up the opportunity?"

"I never wanted to be a princess," I said. "I just wanted to have a pillow that didn't do double duty as my winter coat."

That was the truth too. I guess I wasn't like other girls. I had never even owned a dress, let alone a fancy one. It's not like there was any event I had to dress up for. You don't have to get all sloppy crying over my sorry childhood. It was done and gone. No use looking back and wishing for something I couldn't have.

"I promise you that you can walk down the aisle in anything you want," Hank said, "Even your shorts and t-shirt if you will make me a promise."

I eyed him suspiciously. Hank didn't ask for much, but when he did, guaranteed it was going to make me feel guilty if I didn't do it.

"Will you at least *try on* a real wedding dress? Just to see what it feels like to look like a princess for a few minutes?"

I patted his hand. "If it means that much to you, I will."

We drove most of the rest of the way in silence. If a relationship is measured by the number of words shared, then Hank and I were in trouble. Strange thing is, it was what I liked maybe best about Hank. I never felt like I had to talk. He didn't mind silence, and I found words never said what I wanted them to say. I preferred listening to the wind and the waves over words. That was a language that never confused me. Words did.

Two hours passed before we pulled into a strip mall. Hank parked in front of a store with a fancy script sign that said, "Betsy's Bridal Boutique."

"I like alliteration," I said.

Hank smiled. He hurried over to open my door, but I beat him to it. I was not used to politeness, though I appreciated the effort. Definitely not necessary, but I have to admit, it made me feel like I was someone special.

As soon as we walked in the door that tinkled with two little white bells with lace bows attached to them I felt intimidated. There were rows and rows of frou-frou dresses, all encased in plastic, in varying shades of white. I wanted to shrink into myself, like a turtle. Instead, I grabbed Hank's hand. That gave me a little courage.

A very sleek, tall woman slinked out of nowhere and appeared at our side.

"Hello! Do you have an appointment?" she asked.

Appointment? To buy a dress you need an appointment?

"Yes," Hank said to my surprise, "For Leah Grace at 2:00."

"And you are the bride?" the sleek woman asked me.

I nodded.

She glanced quickly at a black book on the counter. I guess that held the day's appointments, because she put her manicured finger on it, apparently reading my name.

"Here you are," she said, tapping the page.

No, *here* I am. I wanted to say that because I was feeling uncomfortable in this fancy shop filled with frou-frou. I didn't though. Hank squeezed my hand like he was proud of my restraint.

"My name is Debbie. Nice to meet you Leah. I hope we can find something you will like. I set aside some simpler gowns over here. Please, follow me."

Simpler gowns? I glanced at Hank who gave me an encouraging tug. I wanted to ask Debbie where Betsy of the alliterative sign was. Debbie appeared to be all alone in the shop. However, I was side-tracked by the revelation that Hank had called ahead and even already requested simpler gowns for his fiancée who was more used to slopping around in the mud than Betsy or Debbie could ever begin to imagine.

To get to the simpler gowns, we had to pass a few bazillion yards of gauzy, shimmering, glittering, jewel and lace and sequin encrusted billowing material. We reached the far wall of the store where a three-way mirror buttressed a rack with five or six gowns. From what I could tell, there was not a single pearl button, lace, or frou-frou adornment on any of them. She held one up for me.

Silky material flowed from two thin shoulder straps, draped across a v-neckline, tucked into a tiny waist with a single white cluster of delicate flowers at one side, and then tumbled to the floor in lustrous folds that reflected the lights.

"I'll take that one," I said.

Debbie laughed, like I was joking.

"Maybe you should try it on," Hank suggested.

"Maybe," Debbie agreed. "But sir, do you want to see your bride in the dress?"

"No," he said. "I will be right outside if you want me. You are in good hands with Debbie."

I wasn't thrilled he was leaving, but it did make sense that he be surprised by the vision of loveliness I was almost certain to become in that dress. I couldn't believe how quickly I had fallen for the dress. I hoped Hank hadn't unleashed a monster. When I put it on, Debbie said, "It was as if it was made for you."

It didn't need any alteration, which she said was a miracle. Apparently, I was a perfect size two. Who knew??? She asked if I had shoes yet. I stuck out my foot with my old flip-flops.

Debbie scuttled away and reappeared with boxes of shoes. Again, she told me she had some "simple designs" and pulled a pair out that looked a little like my flip flops, except in white satin with a single little flower at the top of the thong section. There was a small heel, but one I felt even I could probably tackle.

I slipped them on. "I'll take these." They were almost as comfortable as my swamp shoes.

All of fifteen minutes had passed, and I ushered Hank in to pay for my wedding outfit and haul it out to the car. Debbie said this was a world record and told Hank he was a lucky man.

"I know," he said, putting his arm around my shoulder.

The jewelry store was a couple of miles down the road. It took twenty minutes to settle on a simple gold band for each of us. Most of the time was spent trying to convince the salesman I really didn't want a diamond ring. He was sure I was newly released from a mental institution. Finally, we had to threaten him to just sell us the gold bands or we would find another store.

"We have the whole day in front of us now," Hank said. "I have one last surprise for you."

"I don't need any more fancy things, do I?" I asked.

He chuckled and pulled me into a travel agency.

"Let's pick a honeymoon," he said.

That took a couple of hours. I honestly didn't care where we went, but Hank and the travel agent wanted to show me pages and pages of choices. In the end, we settled on a cruise to the Bahamas. I tried not to spoil Hank's excitement by refraining from mentioning that while the water was bluer in the pictures than the water just outside our hut, it didn't have our friendly dolphin pod in it.

"You will love the cruise," the agent said, handing us a pile of brochures. "Congratulations."

Our last stop was an early dinner where we laid out all the brochures and Hank showed me all the wonderful things we were going to do and see. It was a short cruise, island hopping in the Bahamas. He showed me where we would get off the boat for an excursion to snorkel. In the picture there were all kinds of beautiful brightly colored fish.

"Are sharks around?" I asked. "Why don't they show the pictures of sharks?"

"Sharks do live in the ocean," Hank admitted, "But the people running the excursion look out for the sharks."

"How many people get eaten by sharks while snorkeling?" I asked, munching on an appetizer called calamari. It tasted a little rubbery, but dipped in the marinara sauce that came with it, the rubbery texture was not unpleasant. Hank promised he would tell me what it was made of when I finished and decided if I liked it or not.

"I don't think anyone gets eaten by sharks or the snorkeling outfit would probably go out of business."

I finished the calamari, and flicked on my phone. I entered "shark attacks while snorkeling in Bahamas" in the search bar. Try it yourself. The first few hits were all about a woman from North Carolina whose arm was bitten off by a shark while snorkeling in the Bahamas.

"She wasn't eaten," Hank said.

"Her arm was."

I scrolled to a site that listed statistics of shark attacks in the Bahama waters. The records which were kept since 1860 showed about 100 attacks.

"That's not very many in 160 years. Less than one a year," Hank said.

"Only one so far this year," I pointed out. "Still, unless the shark has checked this website, there could be a hungry shark just waiting. This calamari is yummy. What is it made from?"

"Squid," Hank said.

I almost choked. I put down my fork.

"I'm nervous about that snorkeling business," I said.

"We don't have to do it if you don't want to," Hank said, pulling me against him. Two little circles of squid looked up at me in what appeared to be an accusatory expression.

"I don't want to spoil your fun."

"It is fun for me to show you things you never had a chance to see growing up. I didn't think you would be worried about sharks since you swim with Flash and Pinky all the time."

"They are not sharks."

"No, but where dolphin are, sharks can be."

"Seriously???" This was not news I was happy to hear at all.

"I never thought of you as a worrier," Hank said.

I considered this statement. I had not been a worrier growing up, which is pretty hard to believe considering the wealth of things that I had every right to be worried about. And maybe that is why I didn't worry. I didn't have time to worry since I was so busy evading death.

"I guess now that I have nothing much to be afraid of, I sort of like it. It's peaceful."

"The Bible talks about worry."

Of course it does. And leave it to Hank to know all about it and work it seamlessly into our conversation. Not that I minded. The more I learned about God, the more I wanted to know. Maybe Hank would reveal something that would be useful in helping Lolita.

"People can be paralyzed by worry and not do what God would have them do," Hank said.

"Do you think God wants me to go snorkeling?" I asked, sorrowful.

Hank laughed, and squeezed my shoulder. He speared one of the two calamari circles left, dipped it in the sauce, and popped it in his mouth. The remaining calamari winked at me.

"No, I think God would have you do what is relaxing and fun for you on our honeymoon. But sometimes we worry instead of doing what we should be doing with God. Do you know the story of Martha and Mary?"

"No. Mary, Jesus' mother?"

"A different Mary. She was Martha's sister and their brother was Lazarus. All three were friends of Jesus."

"I remember Lazarus. He was the one Jesus raised from the dead."

"Right. Well Jesus came to visit Martha and Mary and Martha was busy cleaning the house and preparing the meal for Jesus. Mary did nothing but sit at Jesus feet, listening to what he was saying to her. Martha was upset with Mary because Martha was doing all the work, and Mary was doing nothing to help. She asked Jesus to tell Mary to get up and help her!"

"What did Jesus do?"

"He told Martha she worried about so many things, but only one thing was necessary…and that Mary had chosen the better thing."

"Laziness?" I asked.

"No… she knew Jesus was Lord. She had proclaimed exactly that when Lazarus was sick and died so we know she understood who Jesus was. She was soaking up His words, and listening to Him…being with Him. She chose to be in relationship with Jesus rather than worrying about the cares of the world."

"But the dinner wasn't going to make itself!" I said.

"No…that's true. But in that situation, Mary knew that the most important thing was not the dinner, but the presence of God Himself. And Jesus made it clear that He wanted less of our doing *for* Him than our being *with* Him. I think that's why He said Mary had chosen the better way. He didn't say Martha had chosen a bad way, only that Mary had made the better choice. He wants a relationship with us, and perhaps that is part of the cure for destructive worrying."

I considered this while exchanging glances with the remaining calamari.

"Lolita told me she wants to believe in Jesus."

Hank raised his eyebrows, turning his full attention on me.

"Did she make a profession of faith?"

"No…at least I don't think so. She started crying. She wants to believe, but I don't think she does."

"That is probably a hopeful sign," he said.

"I didn't know what to say to help her," I admitted. "I don't even know why *I* believe. I still have a lot of questions and a lot of doubt."

"The Bible says that they who seek Him find Him. It also says that it is God Himself who opens our eyes, and leads us out of darkness."

"Does God prevent us from finding Him then?" I asked. Frankly, that thought appalled me.

"No. I don't think so. When Jesus was on His way to Jerusalem to be crucified, He sees all the lost people and says how much he longs to gather them into the fold, like a mother hen gathering her chicks safely underwing…but they would have none of it. Later, in 2 Peter 3:9, it says: *The Lord is not slow to fulfill his promise as some count slowness, but is patient toward you, not wishing that any should perish, but that all should reach repentance.*

"See Jesus is waiting to come again, and hold all to account as promised on the day of judgment because He doesn't want ANY to perish. He wants ALL to reach repentance, and know Him, and give their lives to Him. He longs for Lolita to turn to Him."

"I don't know if she will," I said. "She is pretty angry at how unfair her childhood was. It forced her into prostitution…at least the way she sees it."

"The very fact that she wants justice speaks of the truth of the Gospel. Who put that standard of justice in her? And if she knows there was a standard of fairness that she was denied, that sin destroyed her childhood, then she knows how terrible sin is. She wants the scales to be righted, and fairness to be restored, but how does that happen unless someone pays for what was lost to her? When we demand justice as the reason for not seeking God, the huge irony is it is the very proof that God had to exact a penalty for sin. Jesus had to do what He did on the cross for God to provide the just payment for sin. We have to accept His payment or we are still in rebellion against God. We would still rather go our own way than follow the plan God has said is necessary if we are to return to a righteous relationship with Him."

"I'm not sure I could say all that to Lolita," I said after a moment of considering all Hank had said. "I think I understand what you are saying, but I am not sure I could repeat it."

"You don't have to explain it the way I explained it to you," Hank said. "You just have to share why you chose God."

On an impulse, I skewered the remaining calamari, slathered it in the deep red marinara sauce and shoved it in my mouth. It really was delicious if I just savored the flavor and tried not to visualize squids with their long, snaky tentacles.

"Why *did* you choose God?" Hank asked. I was afraid he might try to pin me down on that. Mostly, I wasn't really certain. Did I dare tell Hank that?

"I lived all my life up to this point without Him," I said. "I sure wasn't doing a bang-up job of managing life without God. For sure, my parents weren't. I really had nothing to lose. Well…actually, I did lose some things."

Hank smiled. "Like what?"

"I lost feeling I was all alone. I lost being so miserable and guilty from all the awful stuff I'd done. I lost being afraid that there was a God and when He found me He was going to squash me like an ant."

"And what did you find?" he asked.

"I found you…but besides that I found that I didn't need to run from God any more…that He loved me, and wanted me to be with Him. Like Mary."

"Yes!"

"I can't quite wrap my brain around that, that the same God that created the universe would want to be with me, but I do believe He does."

"I am sure He does," Hank said, "He would not have sent His only son whom He loved so deeply to die a horrific death for us unless He loved us very much."

I nodded, contemplating the incredible wonder of all that.

"Maybe that's what you could tell Lolita," Hank suggested.

11

The next couple of weeks were a flurry of activity. Mom hired a caterer to handle our wedding dinner. We set the date for June 1, and verified that with Pastor Rimerton. Hank and I sat down and worked out an invitation list. It was a short list.

Hank
Me!
Mr. and Mrs. Forrest
Mom
Lolita
Dr Pritchett
Tim
Miss Beam
Miss Mickleburr
William Spear
Mrs. Rimerton and their daughter, Mandy

"That's not very many people," I said.

"They are the most important ones," Hank said.

"Don't you have friends you want to invite?" I asked. Come to think of it, I had never met a single friend of Hank's. Surely, he had church friends, or construction work friends. I realized I had shown a major malfunction in my compassion meter. Why had I never noticed or asked if Hank had friends?

"I never had much time to devote to friends," Hank said. "That was my fault. I felt like it was more important for me to be with my mom when she got sick, and to help my folks with any spare time I had."

I didn't know what to say. It was the first time I realized that the perfect and wonderful Hank had been as lonely and maybe as much a misfit as me. I remembered how our discussion over our Orlando dinner had then moved to the fact that all of us are strangers and aliens in this world. Hank said all of us feel that way, some more than others, but it is based on truth. We are not made for this world. We feel like this is not all there is to life because it was never meant to be all there was to life. We were made for a different world… a world where we would spend eternity with Jesus.

"Besides, a small wedding with our closest friends is exactly what I always wanted," Hank said.

I knew next to nothing about weddings, but Hank told me that he was going to ask Dr. Pritchett to be his groomsman. Was there one of the women I would like as a bridesmaid? He figured my mom would walk me down the aisle since my father was dead. I could hardly restrain a "Praise God" remembering that fact. Had he been alive, he would definitely be walking down the aisle while shooting up some toxic heroin cocktail.

So, who to ask to be my bridesmaid?

"Maybe Lolita," I said. "I have known her the least amount of time…but I think she needs it the most maybe. Besides, I think she likes Dr. Pritchett."

"That sounds kind-hearted of you."

We were sitting on the deck of the fishing hut after dinner. I had progressed to broiling steak and making fresh green beans and rice to go with it. I had a good four or five meals now under my belt. By the time we got married, I should have at least a week's worth of food I could safely provide for my new husband. Zippy sat at our feet, looking at us with an immovable, fixed stare, drool forming a puddle between his paws. I cut off a piece of fat which he dived for.

"What if it rains?" I asked.

"We could set up a tent to be married under just in case." Hank scribbled on his notepad which was our wedding planner.

"Maybe I will go ask Lolita right now," I said. "I need to feed the hawks and Lightning anyway."

"You do that," Hank said. "I will clean up here, and then I need to get going. I will send out invitations tomorrow."

I kissed him goodbye, and headed on down the path to the mobile home. Lightning saw me and instantly nickered and trotted towards me.

I hopped over the fence and greeted her. It had been a long time since we had gone traipsing through the woods along the shore together. Early on when I had first come to Kumsquat, we explored our surroundings nearly every day.

"Let's go hiking," I told her. She nuzzled me in response, and I knew she was on board for an adventure. I scurried to the hawks' enclosure when Lolita popped out of the trailer.

"Hi," she said. "I was wondering when you would be around."

"I was having dinner with Hank," I said.

She nodded and opened the door to the medical shed. As we began spooning out the pieces of chopped up rodents, she sighed. "I am glad you have a normal relationship with a nice man. I am jealous."

I didn't know what to say to that. It boggled my mind that anyone would find me worthy of one second of jealousy.

"Don't get me wrong," she said, "I really am happy for you. After all you went through, it is great that you are finding happiness now."

I decided now was the time to take the plunge. I knew (sort of) where my happiness came from, and unlike what Lolita thought, it wasn't Hank. Hank was great. Totally. But it was so much more than Hank that had changed my world.

"I think it was God that did that."

"Well...ok. Maybe...in the sense that God sent you Hank."

"I mean more than that. God sent me everything. I was a mess when I came here. I had nothing except my anger at my folks and some of their drug money."

Lolita didn't respond. She was filling the two train-wreck hawks' bowls, and then said, "We need to name them more than mama and baby."

"OK. What do you want to call them?"

Lolita considered this while mixing the medication into their chopped-up mice.

"How about Engine and Caboose?"

I shrugged. Those didn't really sound like names to me, but it would not be right for me to tell her that after asking her to name them, especially considering her melancholy mood.

I collected a live mouse from a little cage filled with them. Tim had said we could start giving Goldy live mice and see how he did catching them. I was supposed to toss one in the enclosure and record what Goldy did. What fun!

Lolita finished placing the bowls in Engine and Caboose's cage, and then a whole dead mouse on the floor of Harry's cage. Now she joined me as we watched what Goldy would do to little Mickey.

I could see why in the beginning we would need to supplement. Goldy was fast enough to overtake the mouse, but when he was above him, the mouse made a quick stop and sprinted in the opposite direction. Goldy could not alter his flight nearly quick enough. He didn't crash, but quick changes in direction were not easy for him and he seemed to tire pretty quickly. Soon, he returned to his perch and watched the mouse scampering about searching for a way to make it out of Dodge City but stymied by the plywood all along the bottom of the aviary.

Eventually the mouse tired as well, and made a fatal mistake. He sat down and started cleaning his whiskers, which personally, did not strike me as the smartest thing to do when a hungry raptor was just twenty feet away.

Goldy may have been yet a little wobbly in flight, but he was cunning. He seized his opportunity and snagged the vain little mouse.

"Score one for Goldy!" Lolita said.

Lightning interrupted our celebration with a shrill reminder that I had mentioned a jaunt along the shore.

"Hey Lolita. Have you ever ridden a horse?"

She laughed. "No. I was too busy stealing customer's wallets to make time for riding lessons."

"Want to try? Lightning can carry both of us."

Lolita started to shake her head, but then stomped her foot and said, "All right. I will."

I helped her climb on the second highest fence rung and then walked Lightning to her side.

"Grab her mane, and throw your right leg over her. Hold onto her mane to help pull yourself onto her back."

"Won't that hurt her? Tugging on her mane?"

"No. I used to even steer her by pulling her mane. Go ahead."

Lolita looked a tad terrified, but she followed my instructions and plopped on top of Lightning.

"It's pretty high up in the air up here." She swallowed and gripped the mane till her knuckles were white.

"I'll climb on in front, and you can just hang on to me. Lightning goes slow. It's easy."

I clambered from the fence rail onto Lightning while Lolita shrieked quietly before clutching my waist.

"Now you can just hang on…maybe a little less tightly…" Here I paused to try to breathe and expand my rib cage against Lolita's death grip.

"Sorry. This is much higher than I expected."

"You get used to it. All I will have Lightning do is walk. We won't go far. Just up-shore a little ways. To make her move, you just tap your heels against her. I sometimes don't even have to do that. It's like she reads my mind. Sometimes if I just lean forward, she goes."

I showed Lolita by just shifting my weight forward, and Lightning moved immediately down the driveway. She had missed our rides as much as I had. I was glad for the raptors and the upcoming wedding, but it had put a definite dent in my time with my original group of friends.

Lolita's death-hold on my waist slowly relaxed as she realized that riding Lightning was not much harder than sitting on a rocking chair.

"This is fun, Leah. Thank you."

"You're welcome. Lightning is a good horse to learn to ride on. Nothing much rattles her and she loves everyone."

"When you found her, she was starving and lost, right?"

"She was pretty skinny, and as far as being lost, I don't know. She was content hanging out with me at the trailer. It was almost as though she was there *for* me."

"Is that what you meant when you said that God sent you everything?"

"Partly. Hank couldn't believe I survived all by myself with no money or anything. But it seems like everything I needed, showed up in the nick of time. I think if Lightning hadn't been there, I might have given up and run back home. She helped me feel like I wasn't alone."

"That's how I felt when I crashed on your shore," Lolita said. "I would never have met you all if I hadn't wrecked my boat going too fast around that corner. That crash might be the best thing that ever happened to me."

I was thinking along exactly the same lines. I sure didn't rejoice over my terrible upbringing by addicted parents, but if I hadn't felt the need to run away, I would never have met Lightning, Flash, Zippy, or Hank. I wondered if God always used calamity to bring about good.

"What are your plans now?" I asked. "Hank told me that he should have your boat fixed any day."

"I don't know. I need to get the boat back to Greg. I can't bring it to him. I haven't figured out my next step."

"You don't have to leave if you don't want to. If you feel safe here, Mom likes your company and you have been a big help with the birds. Also, I wondered if you would be my maid of honor?" I didn't add that she would be my only maid, honor or otherwise, since I had no real friends.

I felt Lolita startle. "Maid of honor?" She asked with a chuckle. "Maid of *dis*honor more like it."

I laughed, hoping she was making a joke.

"Of all the people you could ask, why ask me? You hardly know me, and like I said, honor is not a word usually pinned on my chest."

Again, I didn't divulge that she was really only one of three women I could possibly ask, and I hadn't seen the other two in months.

"That's how I felt when Hank asked me to marry him. Of all the normal people in the world he could have asked, why me? I even asked God that. Of all the people whom He could have bothered with…why me? Runaway daughter of a drunk and a druggie, in and out of detention centers for the first two decades of my life, who never paid Him the slightest bit of attention. Why me?"

"Exactly," Lolita said. Then she patted my back. "I didn't mean why *you*. I was thinking why God would bother with most of us…but especially me. If ever there was some irredeemable garbage, it would be me. Second only to Mitch Connor."

She had never mentioned the dirty cop's name, but I was almost certain that was who Mitch Connor was. I filed that away for future reference. Lightning was plodding along close to the thick blanket of reeds along the shore when there was a raucous sound like what you would imagine a pterodactyl flushed out of the prehistoric underbrush might sound like. A huge blue heron flapped its enormous wings, complaining the whole way as it swept low over the river to the opposite shore.

That startled both of us, but especially Lightning. She snorted and swerved, pivoting suddenly towards the road. I grabbed her mane and managed to right myself, but Lolita was listing to the far right. Lightning broke into a trot which had the fortunate result of tossing Lolita back to midline. She clung to me as we both bounced almost right off Lightning's back. Fortunately, she responded to my tugs on the halter rope and resumed walking in the nick of time.

As we settled back down and our hearts slowed to a sustainable rate, Lolita picked right back up where we had left off.

"I can see why God is interested in you. You are young enough to still have a future."

"My mom isn't," I blurted, "And look at what God did to her. I mean, don't repeat this to her, but if anyone was a worthless irredeemable hunk of flesh it was her. I was done with her. I ran away with no intention of ever seeing her again, and no desire to. But I guess it takes a LOT to make God give up."

"I wouldn't bother," Lolita said.

I wouldn't either. I guess that's why I was not God.

"I'm glad He stuck with me though," I said. "In the end, I decided He was worth trusting since He didn't give up when I really would not have blamed Him."

Lolita didn't add anything more to the discussion. I don't know if she was thinking about it, or was being polite and didn't want to damage my faith. The swampy shore was too mucky for Lightning to tread upon, so she meandered up alongside the road. We decided it was best to head back home since the sun was starting to arc down towards the water. As we passed a telephone pole, Lolita gasped. I looked up at the sign posted to the pole and understood her response. There was her face staring back at me, with the message, "Wanted for questioning by Miami/Dade police. Any information, please contact…"

'That no good son of a ##@@#$%%$**&(**!" Lolita swore. "Pardon my French. Now what do I do?"

"The picture is of a blonde," I reminded her, "You are a brunette now. But maybe you need to reconsider talking to William."

"Your cop friend? I can't talk to him especially now. If that piece of crap Connor is posting this, he must have something on me that he can use."

We plodded on in silence. It occurred to me that Mitch Connor must have some reason to believe that Lolita was in the area. Why else would signs be posted this far from Miami. I would ask William if he knew what Lolita was accused of.

"*Could* he have anything on you?" I finally asked.

Lolita didn't answer right away which made me wonder again if she was hiding something. What if she was wanted for something really serious? Like murder? What if I had just asked a murderer to be my bridesmaid? What if everything she had told me so far was a lie, a cover-up?

"I didn't do anything," she said.

"What do you think he is going to say you did?"

"I don't know. Maybe it had to do with my gun."

"Your gun?"

"I had a gun…but not legally. I knew I might need it to protect myself. When I was in his apartment, my gun went missing. I couldn't ask him if he took it since I wasn't supposed to have it in the first place. I suspected he did. I wonder if the ##@@$$%^&*^ creep is framing me for something with the gun."

"Well if it's not registered in your name…how could he frame you?"

She expelled a few more choice words and said, "It has my fingerprints on it. He's a cop…a detective. I imagine he knows that and used gloves when…"

Here she snapped her mouth shut and I realized she knew more than she was letting on. Connor had used that gun, or she had…and maybe she was not ONLY running from a life of prostitution.

12

As soon as we got back home, I fed Lightning and made a quick getaway to my hut. I called William Spear, my cop friend as soon as I walked in the door.

"Hi Leah! I just got the wedding invitation in the mail today! I am excited for you and will be there! Congratulations."

"Thanks William. I have a question. I was riding along Kumsquat Highway and saw a posted wanted sign. It had a picture of someone that I might have seen…maybe in Orlando."

Now this was not totally honest, but was true. I *might* have seen her in Orlando. *Might* was the operative word. *Might* implies there was a possibility and since I wasn't certain she had not been in Orlando beyond a shadow of a doubt, I didn't feel it was a mortal sin to use a word that could be construed as deceptive.

"When?" he asked.

"A few days ago. I went with Hank. I was wondering what she is wanted for."

"Questioning in a murder case. A Jane Doe drug addict. That's all I know. Some information about her being part of a prostitution ring."

"Do they think she did it?" I asked through a suddenly dry mouth.

"I don't think so. I think they believe she ran the prostitution ring."

"Was the ring in Miami?"

"Run out of Miami. This girl was found in a small town north of Miami. There was a tip about this lady on the poster. She was a well-known escort years ago in Miami, and then fell off the radar."

William asked for specifics about where and exactly when we had seen the person of interest. I wondered if I could get in big trouble for leading him astray. I said I wasn't at all certain it was her but wondered if my mom was in any danger living alone now. William assured me they did not think the woman was in the area, but that posters had been distributed all over southern Florida.

"But do they think she is dangerous?" I asked again.

"Only if you are a drug addict runaway," William said. "If she was running a prostitution ring entrapping runaway girls, she is not someone I'd want to chum around with."

Or have as a bridesmaid?

What if everything she had said about Mitch Connor, the dirty cop, was just a cover up? What if she was the one who was doing all the terrible things she blamed him for? I felt sick. How does one figure out who to trust?

The next day, Lolita was subdued as we fed the hawks. Harry only took about fifteen minutes this time to catch the live mouse. He was already steadier in his change of direction while winging his way to breakfast. I jotted notes for Tim. Tim showed up not long afterwards bursting with good news. It turns out the land lease we needed for the new flight cage was approved and we could break ground immediately. The Florida Raptor center was working with local agencies to send construction crews out within the week. This news perked Lolita out of her funk a little.

"How long till the flight cage will be finished?" She asked.

"Oh, if they get the full crew, within a month!" Tim said. "Probably not soon enough for Goldy but maybe for Harry."

"And for sure for Engine and Caboose!" I said.

Tim raised an eyebrow.

"The train wreck hawks," Lolita explained.

"Good names," he said.

"With the flight cage, we will be likely housing eagles from all over south Florida," Tim said. "They hope I will stay on to train new employees." He glanced at Lolita. "No promises about funding for new employees, but they are exploring it. I know you mentioned settling here, Lolita. Is that still in the game plan?"

"I'm not sure," she said.

She didn't add what I was thinking which was the game plan could change if she was arrested for murder. Somehow, I did not believe it was possible Lolita had killed the girl or I would have turned her over to William. Maybe she was just setting me up as a gullible fool with her story about the dirty cop trying to frame her with her illegal gun.

"You'll have some time to think about it," Tim said. "For now, Leah, we need to do some PT on Engine and Caboose. I thought you would like to start learning how to grab a hawk."

I didn't feel at all ready, but Tim felt the juvenile was small enough for me to practice safely on. He went over the procedure in detail while Lolita and I listened.

"I'll be right beside you to help control any body parts you miss," he assured me. "This is the key point. Be confident and don't be tentative. Commit to it fully and go for it."

"He who hesitates is lost," Lolita said.

Tim chuckled. "Yes, exactly. You cannot be wishy-washy grabbing a raptor, even a young injured one. Now remember the leg is still healing so you will want most of your control to be around his breast. I will be right there to control the head. You just do the body grab and firmly hold the legs but don't torque them."

He assured me that Engine would leave us alone, and Caboose was still so wobbly that he was unlikely to put up much of a fight. That turned out not to be totally true. Let's just say I was glad I was wearing goggles and Kevlar gloves. If Tim hadn't been there, it would not have had a happy ending. You don't need any more details than that. Tim told me I did great for my first time, but the evidence was NOT overly compelling in support of that praise, if you ask me.

Tim took over, laying Caboose on his back and while I helped restrain him and keep a covering over his head, Tim showed me how to range the wings to fully outstretched position. We did that a few times and then he did some gentle movements of Caboose's legs. Tim seemed happy with how he was progressing.

He tackled Engine next, and my only job was to cover her head and then while Tim restrained her, I got to range her wings, just like Tim had done with Caboose.

We left the enclosure, after filling their food bowls with some little mice tidbits as rewards.

He told Lolita that she could go in Harry's enclosure and walk along the edge, spooking him to fly from one end to the other five times. Lolita was not at all nervous, which impressed me. The hawk was definitely afraid of her and didn't want to go near her, but still…those talons and hooked beak were awfully sharp and scary looking

"Great job," Tim told her. "You're a natural. Most people are afraid."

I got to do the same thing in Goldy's enclosure. He had a larger flight area, and I was to have him fly back and forth eight laps. Tim took notes, recording his observations and then shared that with both of us. I was impressed by the subtle things he noticed that I would never have considered.

"I've been doing this a long time," Tim said. "You'll start to see more and more the longer you are looking for it."

That line stuck with me. Later, as Lolita and I were sitting in the water cooling off, she mentioned what Tim had said.

"That's true, what he said about the longer you look for things, the more you see what was always there but maybe you never noticed."

I continued looking out at the water, since there was a disturbance of ripples. I hoped it was Flash coming to visit.

"You mean how Goldy was always veering right in her flight because the right wing must be weaker?" I asked.

"Well yes…that too. But I was thinking about what you told me about God, and how a prostitute was an ancestor of Jesus…and how God was always speaking to you and showing you He was there but you didn't always notice. Then one day…you did."

I said that? I didn't quite remember putting it like that, but Hank told me that the Holy Spirit sometimes takes over and we hear exactly what it is God needs us to hear. Maybe this was an example of that.

"I think that might be happening to me. I never saw God at all before coming here."

"Well that's not such a big surprise," I said, "It sounds like you were a little preoccupied running for your life."

"Thank you for that," she said, "But there were signs that I ignored. Last night, I started thinking of them."

I waited, still watching the telltale ripples in the river. I would bet any moment a dolphin would break the surface. The ripples moved further out, but still no sleek grey back or fin emerged.

"When I first ran away, and the first pimp gave me shelter, there was a woman that would stand on the sidewalk outside the building where the girls huddled in a single room. I would pass that woman every day on my way out each night looking for tricks. She always tried to hand me some food. Crackers, a sandwich, a piece of fruit. Sometimes I took it, but I always made fun of her. There was always a note, handwritten and tucked inside the baggie. Jesus 3:16, *For God so loved the world that He gave his only begotten son that whosoever believes in Him should not perish but have everlasting life.*"

Lolita shook her head, and kicked her submerged feet back and forth in the water. "I tossed the little notes on the street. I didn't know if I had the stamina to make it through the night, let alone everlasting life. Then later, when the man who fell for me put me up in a nice apartment, the doorman who surely knew what I was… used to let me in and each time tell me, 'God has a plan for you, a plan and a purpose, plans to prosper and not to harm you.' He told me that was in the Bible. Each new abortion the man forced me to endure I would think of that verse while struggling with the terrible cramps and pain. If that was prospering with God, I sure wasn't interested."

The ripples had disappeared, and I figured I must have been wrong. Maybe it was just the wind, though I had been certain it was Flash or one of his pod members.

"But maybe that was God speaking," Lolita said, "Maybe that was His way of giving me hope. The problem is, I didn't see it as a prophecy, but as a description of what I was supposed to be experiencing then and there. I sure wasn't seeing any purpose or prosperity. Then, when I ran away again, and started to be in hot demand as a high-end call girl, I was definitely prospering…but I doubted making a bundle as a hooker was God's plan or purpose. But one of the men in my apartment building was a pastor. I know he knew what my business was. He saw me with a different guy every night. He never made me feel condemned, even though I knew I was going to Hell, if there was such a place. He used to tell me, 'God bless you, Jesus loves us so much that while we were yet sinners He died for us!' He always said it with a big smile and the kindest expression on his face. I didn't believe in this Jesus or His death for me, but I could tell the pastor believed it and was giving it to me like a gift.

"So I would tell him, 'Jim, maybe Jesus died for you, but He knows He'd be wasting His death on me.' And do you know what Pastor Jim said every time?"

Here she turned to me, expecting an answer apparently. I could not imagine what Pastor Jim said. I shook my head.

"He told me, 'If you were the only one on earth, He would have died for you.' I always thought that was a little over the top. Do you think it is true?"

Honestly, I didn't know, and it was a silly question anyway. She was *not* the only one on earth. Jesus had His pick of sinners to die for. I wracked my brain trying to think if I had read any verse in my Bible that could answer her question.

"Well, I don't know about that, but I know in the story of the lost sheep, Jesus says the shepherd leaves the 99 safe ones to find the one who is lost and doesn't give up till it is found."

"That doesn't sound wise," Lolita said. "He's leaving all those sheep in danger to go after one. If a wolf shows up, the 99 sheep are mutton chops."

I had not really thought of it that way before. "I don't think that is the point of the story. I think Jesus is trying to say that even one lost sheep matters to Him."

"Even a lost sheep that was busy leading those 99 safe ones astray?"

"Maybe *especially* that one," I said.

"Well, whatever…any way about it the fact that Pastor Jim would tell me that every time he saw me was comforting in a strange way. I didn't believe Jesus died for me, nor did I want Him to…but the fact that Jim thought I was worth dying for meant a lot to me. Maybe it gave me hope and I didn't even know it."

Now here I could really relate. I totally understood that feeling of worthlessness. I also was very surprised and resistant to the idea that anyone, let alone GOD would die for me. My parents had definitely made it clear to me that a quarter ounce of meth was worth more than I was to them.

"It doesn't seem fair that Jesus had to bite the dust so I could live," Lolita said.

"No. It isn't," I agreed. "That bothered me too. But He already did it. It's not like He could take it back. Here's what Hank told me about that. If God created us, then He has every right to decide what we have to do to be allowed in His presence. He has the right to decide we have to be punished for sin, and He gets to set the punishment. He also gets to decide if He wants to offer to pay the penalty for us or not. No one else could have done that. If God is the law-creator, then God gets to call the shots in who is allowed to pay the penalty sin demands."

"He could have decided not to have any penalty for sin and then no one has to die," Lolita said.

"That's true. But would it be heaven if that dirty cop who is after you stays just as evil as he is now and he gets to go to heaven without repentance or payment for his sin…after what he did to you?"

She looked stricken. I kicked myself for bringing him up again.

"No," she whispered, "I don't want God to let him in at all. If he accepts that Jesus died on the cross for him, does he get to go to heaven too?"

I knew this was one of those questions that no matter how you answer you are doomed. She was not going to like any answer I gave. I decided to go with the truth, as best I knew it, which admittedly was probably naïve and not without error.

"The Bible says that *whosoever* believes that Jesus is Lord shall not perish…but have everlasting life."

"Then I don't want to go to heaven. Not if he's going to be there. I had all I can stand of him here on earth."

Oh Hank, where are you when I need you?

"Heaven's a big place. Maybe you wouldn't run into him," I said.

Lolita burst out laughing.

"Honestly," I said, "I get what you are saying. If my dad is in heaven, I might just jump off the cloud. But before my mom came here, before she knew God, I would have said the same thing about her. He really did change her. I mean, I actually *want* her to be here now. I never would have believed it."

"Leah, you are a really sweet girl, and I appreciate all the effort you are taking to tell me about God. But honestly, I couldn't say I accepted Jesus' offer just to get into heaven. I'd have to really believe it and all it means to follow Jesus and all the list of things I have to do to be right with God. I am not sure I have it in me."

"I don't either," I said. The irony is I said that because I didn't want to lie, since the Bible says 'thou shalt not lie', and so I was admitting I could not abide by God's standards in telling the truth and thus abiding by God's standards. Must be the Holy Spirit Hank was trying to tell me about.

"But you are a Christian, right?"

"Yes…I mean I did ask Jesus to be Lord of my life, and I do want to live for God…but I blow it more than I really want to let on. But there is a difference. I don't WANT to blow it, and I am instantly sorry when I do. That's new."

"You don't have to be perfect?" she asked.

"I sure hope not."

The ripples reappeared and this time, Flash's fin sliced through the surface. Lolita gasped and drew back her feet.

"It's just Flash," I said. "He won't hurt you. I think he's been there the whole time we were talking."

"How do you know?"

"I know the signs. The ripples are different when the dolphins are just under the surface."

I thought about that with a wave of clarity. I had learned to know the dolphins were there even when I couldn't see them. I could see evidence of their presence even when they were hidden. I wasn't sure, but thought maybe the Holy Spirit was sending me an insight. I hoped Lolita was getting the same insight because we wouldn't have time to discuss it.

Mitch Connor's motorboat had just rounded the bend in the river and his face was pointed in our direction, as was a gun.

13

This was definitely NOT GOOD. Lolita did not scream. At least I don't think she did. I can't be sure since I was screaming too loudly to hear her.

"Shut up," Connor said. "I could care less about you. I am after her."

He pointed the gun at Lolita. I was so scared I didn't even point out that technically, he probably meant to say "I *couldn't* care less about you." It is a common mistake and makes me want to throttle the people who say it. I didn't think now was the time for a grammar lesson.

"You looked better as a blond," he said to Lolita.

"You looked better five hundred miles away," she said.

Personally, I would not have insulted the person whose finger was poised on a trigger, but that's just me.

"We're going for a little ride," he said.

Now, maybe you, like me, as we were beginning to think this through, realized the danger. Not only was he probably planning on taking Lolita somewhere where he could strap on some cement shoes and let her find her way back from the bottom of the ocean, but he would at some point realize I could identify him. That definitely did not bode well for my future as a bride in a few weeks. Not a living one, anyway.

Lolita decided to play hard to get.

"For what? I got a nice comfy place right here you could...rest." She winked and tossed her head such that her hair draped over one eye. I knew what she was up to, stalling for time and playing the coy hooker card. I also figured that Connor would not be so stupid as to fall for it.

I was wrong. He looked at her with the same stupid expression I used to see on my neighbor's hound dog when he got scent of a female dog in heat. However, the foggy look shifted as he shook his head.

"You're under arrest," he said.

She laughed, though her eyes darted at me in fear. "For what? Wasting my time with you?"

"Possession of a stolen weapon used in a murder."

"I don't have a weapon."

"We have retrieved the weapon. Your fingerprints are all over it. It was used in the murder of Jane Doe, a sixteen-year-old addict in Miami."

Well, she had known this was coming. Now, did she do it or was she being framed as she claimed? I wished that the famous Holy Spirit Hank had told me would guide me in all wisdom would guide me now. Not that it would do any good. What would I do with all that wisdom? I wasn't holding a gun, and even if I were, it wasn't likely the trained cop would let me use it to send him off to a time-out corner.

"I haven't been to Miami in ten years," she said.

"Then your fingerprints traveled there all by themselves," he said.

He tossed an anchor over the edge of the hull while keeping the gun trained on Lolita. He was in very shallow water. I guessed he intended to climb down the little ladder off the side of the boat, wade over and haul Lolita into the boat.

"I know what you're doing," she said.

"I'm arresting you."

"You're framing me. I know you stole my gun, and I know all about your little side business. I know you killed that girl yourself, probably because she was threatening to expose you."

I can't tell you how fervently I wished she hadn't said all that. If it was true, any pretense of him legitimately hauling her off to jail was gone, and I was now the other pair of eyes he had to drown.

He must have come to a similar conclusion because he glanced at me quickly. I could see him sizing me up to determine what size burlap bag he'd need to wrap my body in.

He was still mulling over exactly how best to stuff both of us on his boat when Lolita added another little bit of lead to my skull.

"And Leah here knows all about it."

I turned to Lolita blinking in astonishment. I was about to let loose with a few choice words from my pre-Christian days, when she tossed me a quick wink. So quick I almost didn't catch it. She was up to something. I was to play along. Maybe the Holy Spirit was talking to me.

"Leah's best friend is a cop. Lucky for me! The day I arrived running from you when I saw that murdered girl on the news. I knew where I had seen her before. At your place. It didn't take much to figure out she was another of your homeless addicts you turned into a whore."

"She was always a whore…just like you. I just made sure she was paid."

"Yeah, paid by dying."

"That was an accident!" he snapped. He immediately gasped and looked at me again. The jig was clearly up. I was destined to be fish food within an hour.

"Both of you. Get in the boat."

"I didn't finish telling you about Leah's cop friend," Lolita said, smirking.

(FYI, 'smirk' is one of those words very overused particularly by two-bit authors who have a limited vocabulary, but there are some precious few moments when smirk is a good choice. This is one of them.) I was *not* smirking, on the other hand. I was wondering how long I could hold my breath in case I was still alive when he tossed me in the middle of the river.

"He took a statement from me and I handed over all the photos I've collected over the years of every one of those girls who came to your place, and every note you made in your little black ledger about who was meeting who in what sleaze ball hotel. We can get in your boat, but there's an APB out on you now. I imagine Leah's cop friend is going to put two and two together when both of us are missing."

"You're lying," he said. He did not say it with the same confidence he'd had when he had first been pointing the gun at her head.

"His name is Officer Spear," I said, "Maybe you would like to call and ask if Lolita's lying," I said.

"Lolita?" Connor scowled at Lolita, and then cackled like a mad goose. "That's so unoriginal, Robin."

Robin? Well, now I understood the comment long ago when we met her about being named after a bird. I hoped her name was all she'd lied to us about.

"OK, *Lolita*…you and Leah, stand up."

He motioned with his gun at both of us. He started down the ladder of the boat, still keeping his beady eyes and the gun barrel steadied on us. We stood up. With his free hand he gripped the ladder rail and lowered himself into the water. It only came up to his knees.

"To the ladder. Now." He motioned with the gun again back and forth between our skulls which I quickly figured out was his way of saying if we didn't comply one or both of us were losing our craniums.

Lolita…AKA Robin….shot a beseeching look at me filled with fear. If she was thinking I had any idea of how to get out of this mess, she was in for a shocker.

"If we're not lying," I said quickly, "You know Officer Spear is already looking for you."

"If you're not lying, I'm already in trouble," he said.

"But not for murder," I said.

"Well actually *yes* for murder," Robin reminded me, thinking of the Jane Doe addict.

I rolled my eyes, and Robin recognized her error. "Oh. Sorry."

"Go," growled Connor.

We shuffled slowly through the water to the ladder. Connor stepped back, keeping the gun pointed at our heads but moving out of any range where we could hope to do something desperate like try to shove him, force his head underwater, and wrestle the gun away. Hey…a girl can dream, can't she?

Robin was in the lead and two rungs up the ladder with me right behind her. I paused, glancing back at the field. Once, my dear Lightning had saved me from a similarly nasty man. She had kicked his skull at just the perfect moment and saved the day. Sadly, right now she was indeed watching us, but behind the closed gate of her fenced pasture. No miraculous set of perfectly timed hooves were going to be crunching any brittle head bones today.

On other occasions, it was Zippy who had saved the day. It was completely unlike Zippy not to be on my heel. Then I remembered he'd been sleeping on my bed when I'd headed over to meet Tim for our hawk training session. Zippy was still in the little hut. No canine crusader to our rescue either. He was snoring away nestled on my pillow, oblivious to the watery fate that awaited me.

You know how they say your life flashes before your eyes when you are in your last moments? That was what I experienced then as I slowly trudged up the ladder after Robin. I remembered growing up with my drugged-out pop and drunken mother and how I dreamed one day of escaping to a life where bedtime was not accompanied by the rattling snores of their comatose bodies stretched out on the floor. I remembered stepping over that well-worn scenario, careful not to nudge and awaken them with my backpack stuffed with their drug money and one extra set of clothes, then making my way to the bus station, and buying a one-way ticket out of Hell. I remembered landing in Florida, and hitching my way to Kumsquat, the middle of nowhere which is exactly where I wanted to be where no one would know or find me. I remembered stumbling across the rusty old trailer without a door and busted windows and settling there thinking is was as good a place to hide as any. And then Lightning found me and befriended me, and then Zippy, and Hank, and Flash.

As soon as I thought of Flash, I felt a whoosh of water against my legs. I don't know why I had forgotten Flash until that moment. I swung around in time to see the streak of his grey body zoom right into the legs of Mitch Connor who keeled over like a bowling pin. If he wasn't dead, he probably wished he was judging from the force of the impact and the snap that sure sounded like a femur splitting in half. The gun spiraled into the air and splashed down somewhere in the deeper water several feet behind the boat.

Some gurgling sounds alerted me to where his body was settling underwater. I did NOT initially rush to save him. Sue me. It was not the gurgling and slight flailing of arms sinking underwater that prompted me to reach into my compassionate nature for all humankind, even murderous dirty cops who deserved to die. It was the sound of car doors slamming, and then William Spear and Dr. Pritchett shouting and running towards us.

I hopped off the boat ladder, and waded over to the partially submerged body of Connor. Grabbing his arm, I struggled to pull him to shore. As soon as his face broke the surface, he sputtered to life and, in his gratitude, tried to shove a fist in my face.

Fortunately, I was in better shape at that moment than he was and managed to duck in time. By then, William was upon us, and I backed off. I was probably in a little bit of shock because I splashed down on shore and let William take over. By the time, I looked up again, Flash was gone, Robin/Lolita was kneeling beside me, and Connor was being told he had the right to remain silent.

He had the *right* to remain silent but that was amplified by his *inability* to speak since he was puking up swamp water, and clutching at a leg that was definitely not supposed to bend in the direction it was bending.

14

So maybe you are wondering how William happened to show up in the nick of time. *That*, I can explain. What I can't quite explain is how Flash showed up. It was really Flash that had saved our lives.

While the ambulance medics were loading the pathetic Connor into its back, Lolita/Robin was full of questions.

"How did you know to show up!?"she asked William.

He glanced at me and raised an eyebrow. I nodded. May as well spill the beans.

"Leah called me last night. She didn't want to divulge your confidence, but she knew that if Connor had posted those signs here, he probably knew you were here. She assumed what you had put in the PO box was the evidence against him, and she knew you'd given a key to Dr. Pritchett. She begged me to look at the evidence that she hoped would clear your name, and help us collar him. I had to get a warrant first to open that box without your permission. Given that you were wanted by Miami PD, that was not an issue. Just like you had told Leah, the evidence you'd collected was enough to arrest Connor on sex trafficking and even abduction of some of those girls. Now, attempted murder will be added to the charges. I suspect Connor will be looking at a lifetime of bars in front of his face."

"And me....?" Lolita/Robin paused.

"You have nothing to worry about ma'am. It is obvious from your evidence what Connor was doing, as well as his involvement with the deceased Jane Doe. The local detectives have already gotten statements from some of the girls implicating Connor."

"What will happen to them?" She asked.

"We have rehab centers that will work with victims of the sex trade," William said. "Those girls will get the help they need."

"What hit him?" Lolita asked. She looked out at the water. I realized then she had never seen Flash. "I mean one minute he's got a gun pointed at my head, and next moment I hear a crack like a big tree limb breaking off and he's underwater and the gun is splashing down twenty feet away."

"That was Flash," I said.

"The dolphin?" Lolita/Robin said

William shook his head, grinning. "Those crime fighting animals at it again. Next thing you know we are going to have to promote them and get them a badge."

"The dolphin IS dangerous, then?"

"No…only to bad guys. He's never harmed anyone else."

"How did he know Connor was bad?"

"I don't know," I said. "But dolphins are supposed to be highly intelligent. He did always warn us when Connor was near. Maybe he sensed our fear."

"Well there was plenty of that," Lolita/Robin said.

"I am Officer Spear, by the way," William said, extending his hand to Lolita/Robin. "I guess we never really met."

"I'm Loli….Robin. Robin Lark."

I wondered if Lark was really her last name. She smiled at me, reading my mind.

"Yes, my last name really is Lark. My mom always said it was like killing two birds with one stone with my name. I probably could have done a better job of coming up with an alias…I loved Nabokov's novel, Lolita. As you can probably guess if you ever read it…I could relate to Lolita. It seemed fitting."

Nabokov? How many hookers do you think have read Nabokov?

"I know what you're thinking," Robin said, glaring at me, "Just because of…my past…it doesn't mean I was stupid."

I nodded. Chastened. She was almost as good at reading my thoughts as that dolphin was.

"I figured Connor would never think I'd use a name that was like a marquis sign pointing to call-girl. Maybe I am stupid. He did find me after all…"

"We got a tip from someone who'd seen you," William said. "That's how he found you. He was the Miami detective on the case."

She shook her head. "I guess he figured no one would believe me if it came to my word against his."

"And he had the gun with your prints, which he used to shoot Jane Doe."

"Why did he shoot her?" Robin asked.

"One of her friends told the police Jane Doe was going to blackmail him. The friend told her not to try it, that she'd end up dead."

"No one would listen to a hooker over a cop," agreed Robin, "That's why I ran."

"Especially a drug addict," William said. "But you were smart, Robin. At least you collected evidence you could use against him. I wish you'd come to us."

She looked down, a troubled look crossing her face. Robin was still holding back. Some secret remained that she was not willing to share, even with Connor in a broken twisted heap on his way to the slammer.

Her look changed when there were more car doors slamming shut and we all looked up to see Dr. Pritchett striding across the field toward us.

"Lolita…Leah…are you both okay?"

"Robin," she said.

Dr. Pritchett swiveled his head, looking for a robin, perhaps another one crashing into my trailer.

"Robin is my name," she said. "I'm sorry I wasn't truthful. I was running for my life. From him." She jerked her head in the direction of the ambulance. The medics closed the rear doors and waved as they climbed into the ambulance.

"I need to go process the arrest," William said.

Dr. Pritchett looked back at Robin. "Who? What happened? Why were you running from someone?"

Robin heaved an enormous sigh. Dr. Pritchett had not been told any part of her life I suspected. I didn't envy her fessing up now. Hank had always told me that confessing our sins to God was liberating. He admitted that it was painful too, but necessary for healing. I hoped Dr. Pritchett had as forgiving a heart as he seemed to. Robin's own heart was in for some trampling if he didn't.

The ambulance siren drowned out her first few words, and she fell silent.

After a few flurried questions which I tried to answer without exposing Robin's secrets, I sputtered to silence as well. I was a little worn out from almost dying to have the energy to hedge damaging revelations. Let Robin handle it.

"How about you tell me over lunch?" Dr. Pritchett said. "We break ground on the new flight cage tomorrow. The land lease was approved instantly. Tim is enthusiastically endorsing we hire you on as a part-time employee if you are willing. Not immediately. In a month. He plans to train you while the flight cage is being built."

"Maybe you want to hear my story before you decide if you want to hire me." She looked down and her eyes glistened.

Dr. P reached for her hand. "I would like to hear your story." Always a gentleman, he turned to me. "Would you join us for lunch too, Leah? I guess there is a big story I know nothing about."

"I can't," I said. "After I take care of the birds, Hank is coming by. We are meeting with Pastor Rimerton for the wedding plans…going over what I want for the ceremony."

This was true, but it wasn't for a few hours yet. Somehow, maybe the Holy Spirit was talking, I decided it was best that Robin have the lunch-time discussion alone with Dr. Pritchett.

"I need to change out of my wet clothes," Robin said.

She dropped Dr. P's hand which we both noticed she'd still been holding. Hurrying off to the trailer, she shot me a grateful look.

"Do you know her story?" he asked me.

I nodded, wincing. I sure didn't want to be the one to destroy Dr. P's feelings for Robin. It was clear he had them.

Dr.P looked over at the hawks. All three of them were watching us.

"I spend my entire days working with wounded creatures," Dr. P said quietly. "I guess given all that time healing broken bodies, I have a sense when there is a wounded spirit. I always knew Lolita…Robin…had a sorrowful background. I just didn't know the particulars."

"I didn't either," I said. "I still probably don't. I hope she will tell you everything."

"Am I going to be shocked?" he asked.

"I was," I admitted. "But I didn't like her any less. Honestly, I liked her more. After all she's been through, it's pretty amazing she isn't hateful. I probably would be."

"It can go either way with deep wounds," Dr. Pritchett said. "There are some birds that are so shell shocked by the extent of damage they never recover. Even if the wound heals, they don't do well. The trauma to their spirit must be too much to overcome. Then there are others that almost seem motivated by extensive damage. They have a fighting spirit and the wounds just ignite that. I can't always tell which way the creature will respond. Lolita…Robin…is a survivor."

"Yes," I agreed.

"I am glad she had a kindred spirit for a friend," he said, smiling at me.

Me? I probably blushed. I could feel pink warmth in my cheeks.

"I should have asked you first about the Florida Raptor center hiring her part time. Is that all right with you if she agrees to the job?"

"She'll probably be in charge in a few months," I said. "She has a way with birds."

"Yes, she does."

I wouldn't have minded if he had challenged my thought that Lolita…Robin… would be snatching my job out of my hands in a few months, but he didn't. No danger of over-inflating egos here. Really, it was okay. I liked the idea of someone who would be a capable helper in my work, especially as we had new patients fly in. I was enjoying her presence while Tim taught us how to work with the raptors. I realized I had NEVER had a female friend. Robin was perhaps the closest I'd ever come to that.

"She told me you asked her to be your bridesmaid," Dr. P said. "It touched her deeply. She said you were the first woman who had ever sought her friendship. I suspect others were jealous of her."

If he only knew…

"She also said you were the first person who ever answered her questions about God in a way that made her want to know Him. She said if He was your God, maybe she'd be willing to give Him another look."

That surprised me! My stumbling inadequate uninformed answers made her want to seek God? How unlikely was that!??

Robin came out of the trailer now, her dark hair in a high ponytail swinging like a flag in the breeze behind her.

"Ready," she said stepping into the silence. I suspect she knew we'd been discussing her. You can always tell. She looked at each of us quickly. "I'm ready to celebrate freedom. I feel like I just got an *out of jail free* card."

Dr. P laughed. "Well, I can't wait to hear that story."

He tipped his head at me and the two of them walked to his car. I mumbled a brief prayer because I thought Robin would need some added courage. When they'd pulled away, Lightning nickered, stretching her neck across the fence.

I know she had a special sense about when danger lurked and if she could have gotten out of the fence, she would have when Mitch Connor was apprehending us. Now she was calling to me to let her be sure I was well. I hurried over and unlatched the gate. Immediately she stepped out and shoved her nose into my belly, rubbing the full length of it up and down. I threw my arms around her beautiful head.

She nestled against me, blowing warm air into my tummy. That was one of my favorite sensations on earth. As I scratched her behind her ears, she leaned so hard against me that I almost toppled. My thoughts settled on Robin and the shame over her past that she would now be baring to Dr. P. I wondered if she would have the courage. It was as obvious as a tick on a hairless chihuahua that she liked him.

While musing over how that lunch was going, Hank arrived. He hopped out of his truck and told me he had passed an ambulance with a siren blaring on the way over. Kumsquat is a sleepy, nothing-happening kind of town. A blaring ambulance was cause for all kinds of speculation.

"You will never believe what you missed," I said.

Part way through the story, when I relayed details about the gun pointed at my head, Hank threw his arms around me and crushed me against him.

He must have said ten times, "I am so glad you are all right. Oh Lord! Oh Lord!"

I would have answered except he was hugging me so hard I couldn't breathe, let alone expand my lungs to suck in enough air to talk. It may have been my muffled gags that finally helped him loosen his grip.

I finished the story, with less details that might set him off to a strangle hug again. "I feel sorry for Robin," I said, "Having to tell Dr. P who idolizes her about her real background. She looked ashamed…and scared."

"He will forgive her if I know Dr. P. There is a great story of forgiveness that I just read today. In all my readings of the Bible, I had never really noticed it before."

I leaned against Lightning, absently stroking her chest. That was interesting. I figured Hank had the whole Bible memorized. How could he have missed any story inside those cherished pages?

"It's in the book of Mark. Mark is the only one of the four Gospels that tells this detail. It happens in the garden of Gethsemane when Jesus is being arrested. All the disciples flee and melt away in fear. Chapter 14 describes one young man wearing only a linen cloth who runs away naked, leaving the linen cloth behind. Nothing is said about the young man except that. Most people think it was Mark himself."

"That's an odd detail to mention," I said.

"Yes. Exactly. And so it must have significance. Why do you think it is there?"

"I have no idea. I guess his fear of going down with Jesus overcame his shame."

"That's probably true. But think of the importance of the symbol of being naked. Remember in the Garden of Eden, before the Fall when they disobeyed God, Adam and Eve were naked."

"I do remember. And they were not embarrassed. Not till after they sinned. Then they were ashamed and covered up."

"Right. Nakedness became a symbol of shame. Sin exposed the rebellious heart, and they were naked before God in all their sin."

"So the young man ran while Jesus was being led to the cross…where He was going to die for sin."

"That's right," Hank said nodding. "And in abandoning Jesus, his nakedness, his sin, was exposed."

"Why do people think it was Mark? He could have said so…"

"He could have. By keeping the young man anonymous, it makes it easier to generalize the message though. It could have been any young man. The point was he fled from the cross in his nakedness, sin, and shame."

"But you said it was a story of forgiveness."

"Yes. If that was the last we heard of the young man, it would be a sad and incomplete story. The young man could really have done nothing worse than denying his allegiance to Jesus. Like Peter who denied Jesus three times during the arrest and trial before the crucifixion. But in both those instances, a picture of redemption follows."

"I know about Peter," I said. I was becoming a regular theologian, if you ask me! I knew that Peter denied he ever knew Jesus three times before "the cock crowed" just like Jesus said he would. I also knew that when Jesus rose from the dead, He asked Peter three times if he loved Jesus. He gave Peter three chances to publicly admit his love and counter those three public denials. That story always made me happy.

"Well the young man appears again, in Mark 16. But before I tell you about that, here is a really cool detail. The linen cloth the young man was wearing was a sindon…going back to the Greek in the earliest translations. That word occurs just four times in the Bible. The other three times described the linen cloth used in Christ's burial. So the linen cloth left behind by the naked young man is linked to the death of Christ. The covering was removed…and the sin…which Christ died for was completely exposed."

"That's cool," I said. "I mean symbolically cool. Not cool in terms of the sickness of humanity."

"Very," Hank agreed. "And the young man is mentioned again when the two women come running to the tomb where Jesus had been laid…and find it empty! Sitting on the right side of the place where He had been laid is the young man."

"Is he still buck naked?"

"No," Hank said laughing, "He is dressed in a white robe. And he is the first messenger who tells the women that Jesus is risen. He is the first one to explain the significance of the empty tomb. His clothing suggests full restoration before God – first of all, white, and also a robe that completely covers his sin and shame. Or his nakedness. AND he is given the incredibly important job of being the first witness of the risen Christ. He is fully forgiven and restored."

I sighed. "I love happy endings."

"Me too," Hank said drawing me into the circle of his arms.

15

"Go ahead, Leah," Dr. Pritchett said, handing me a shovel. "You can break the first bit of flight center ground. You have earned it."

Hank nodded, with a goofy proud smile. Dr. P stood next to Robin. From what I could tell, their lunch discussion had gone well. He looked, if possible, even more stuck on her than ever. Mom and Tim stood in the circle of well-wishers, along with Mr. Forrest and a crew of muscular young men who would be doing the construction work once this symbolic first clod was unearthed.

I took the shovel. I wondered who to thank for this unexpected miracle. A $20,000 donation was out of the reach of most Kumsquat inhabitants. But why would a stranger build us a flight cage? None of us knew. The folks out at Florida Raptor Center knew but were under strict instructions to keep the donor anonymous.

If I were doing something as awesome as that, I would want others to know. Hank and I had been discussing that just the night before. Hank told me that some people pretended to be humble but whoever our donor was really *was* humble. And humility, he reminded me, was much coveted by God.

"Why?" I asked.

"Well the opposite of humility is pride, and pride did the entire human race in. It was pride that started Satan's rebellion against God in the first place."

"Satan wasn't always bad?" I asked.

"No, the Bible says he was perfect when he was created. There's a passage in Ezekiel describing him and it says: *You were perfect in your ways from the day you were created, till iniquity was found in you.*"

"He was perfect, hanging out with God…why would he want to leave?"

"You could really ask that of anyone, including Adam and Eve. We all have the opportunity to remain perfect in God but none of us seem to be be able to do so. Most of us don't even want it, until we know Jesus. And the Bible tells us the answer to your question. Later in Ezekiel, it says Satan's heart was lifted up because of his beauty."

"Beauty? The devil?"

"He is described in other verses as Lucifer, which means *bearer of light*. It is part of his ability to deceive and destroy. No one expects evil out of beauty."

Bearer of light. That was disturbing that a being designed to be the bearer of light would end up being the guardian of Hell. What made him think that was preferable to perfection with God??

"So, he was proud of being beautiful and became the worst thing to ever happen to us?" I asked. "You know…that makes me think of Robin."

"I don't think of Robin as evil," Hank said. "I think she led a sinful life, but I think she is sorrowful over it."

"No…I agree. What I mean is she is probably the most beautiful lady I have ever seen, but she doesn't seem to be snooty about it. She even has downplayed it here."

Hank thought about this, as though it were some great revelation. It wasn't. Anyone who knew Robin would agree.

"She doesn't seem prideful at all and she has every right to be about her knock-you-down-gorgeous looks," I said.

"Well she didn't do anything but inherit the genetic code for gorgeous," Hank said. "It's not like she had any control over her looks or any right to be puffed up about it."

"Well then none of us have any right to be proud of anything. I mean we all inherit the code of who we are."

"I don't know about that," Hank said, "I think most of us have to be *taught* how to be selfless and kind. Given our own predisposition, most of us would choose our needs over others. But Satan's pride was exactly what we are talking about, I think. His beauty came from His creator and he had nothing to do with it. Still, he says he would be like the most high in Isaiah 14:14. That passage is where he says he will ascend above the stars and be like God."

"I guess you don't get much more prideful than that," I said.

"In a way, every time we disobey God we are saying exactly the same thing," Hank said, "I know better than God…I will be God in my life and choose my own way even if it defies God."

I mused about this for awhile. It made wandering from God sound even more diabolical than I had thought. If our little forays out of God's will made us resemble Satan, maybe I could see why Jesus felt the only recourse was a gruesome death on the cross to pay the cost sin racked up.

"Any time you want to take that first shovel-full will be great," my mother said, interrupting my thoughts about the humble donor and the fall of Satan.

"Should I say a prayer first?" Hank said.

That was totally Hank-like. I wish I had thought of it.

"Yes," I said, "Please do."

All of us lowered our heads and closed our eyes, even Robin. I know that because I peeked. I hope that wasn't a sin, particularly in light of my day-dreaming about the father of sin.

"Dear Lord," Hank said, "We thank you for this day and for this new flight cage and for the donor who made this possible. You know who that is and we pray he or she will be richly blessed. I pray for all the beautiful creatures you created who will be helped by this place where they can strengthen their wings and fly just as you created them to do. Amen."

I gazed at Hank. What a perfect prayer. Robin swiped away a tear that had dribbled down her cheek.

I thrust the shovel into the ground and pulled up a good-sized chunk of rick dark swamp dirt. Everyone clapped. I tossed the dirt to the side and noticed an earthworm sail through the air.

"Now we get to work," Tim said, taking the shovel from me. The construction workers all swarmed together, gathering in groups and pulling out plans and supplies from nearby trucks, lined up along the edge of the field. The brief celebration evaporated in busy workers attacking their designated duties.

Tim told me he needed to X-ray the two train wreck hawks and it would be a great chance for both Robin and me to learn how to operate the machine and handle the hawks for that procedure.

"That sounds fun!" Robin said.

Hank took my hand and we all followed Tim across the street. Zippy was happily trotting at my heel. Mom offered to put him in the trailer so he wouldn't freak the hawks out while they were being caught and subdued.

As she was gathering him up, a car pulling an empty boat trailer turned the bend in our quiet road and slowly approached. It stopped at my driveway. I was already by the aviary, and couldn't see the driver with the glare of the sun on the glass. The man rolled down his window. Robin gasped, and I wondered if Connor had somehow escaped. It wasn't Connor. I could see that even from where I stood. Another startling thing I could see, and probably what Robin could see that had caused her to cry out was that a young girl sitting in the passenger seat was the spitting image of Robin. There was little doubt about who that child's mother was.

Dr. Pritchett seemed to reach the same conclusion, and his eyes opened wide. Apparently, judging from his response, the lunch with Robin yesterday had not aired *all* the dirty laundry. He seemed as shocked by this little clone of his beloved as we were.

"Robin has a daughter?" Tim asked. We all shook our heads and shrugged.

"Is that her husband?" he said.

"I don't think she's married…but I don't know who he is," I said.

"Bet a million dollars her name is Melanie," Mom said.

We would find out. The man pulled into the driveway. He and the girl got out of the car. Robin still had not moved. Her face was pale, her eyes wide and transfixed on the child. The girl did not act like she was being reunited with her mother. In fact, she stood politely as though meeting a stranger. There was little doubt that she had never met Robin before, judging from the responses of both her and Robin.

Finally, Robin spoke. "Greg. How did you know where to find me?" Her eyes never left the girl's face.

Greg! I remembered that name. The man who had befriended Robin, and loaned her the boat. The boat that was fixed now. I had wondered when Robin intended to return it.

"It was all over the news about Mitch Connor. The story about him trying to abduct you and another young lady. How he was injured and apprehended, and evidence of his role in that poor teen's death. I knew he was no longer a threat."

He glanced at the girl beside him.

Robin approached slowly. All the rest of us stared in stunned silence. She kneeled in front of the little girl.

"You're pretty," the girl said.

"Melanie," Greg said, "This is Robin. She's my friend I wanted you to meet."

Robin held out her hand, and gently clasped Melanie's small fingers. "I have wanted to meet you for a long time."

"Daddy says you have our boat. He told me we could take it for a ride with you. That we had so much to talk about!"

Robin looked up at Greg. I had the feeling he was arranging a meeting she had not been informed about. I had a million questions. How had Melanie, who looked eleven years old or so, never met her mother? And why had Robin kept her identity a secret from her own daughter? What did Connor being caught have to do with the timing of this meeting? Why was Robin crying?

I knew why Dr. Pritchett looked like he was ready to cry. I am pretty sure he figured Greg was the father of Melanie and there was NO doubt who the mother was. Unless Robin had lied to me about Greg as well, he was not the father. Whoever the father was, it was clear that Robin had managed to save this one child from the sad fate of her other unborn babies.

"I would like that," Robin answered Melanie. Now she turned to Greg, standing up. "Greg, these are my friends who protected me when I ran from Connor." She introduced each of us in turn.

When she introduced Hank, he pointed to the newly repaired boat, near the shore.

"There's your boat. I can help you load it onto your trailer."

"Thanks," Greg said, "I'd appreciate that. I don't mean to interrupt your day. I really mostly wanted to be sure Robin was safe and it was a nice drive for Melanie and me. I wasn't even sure I'd find the place. I'd never heard of Kumsquat before."

"If you have time now," Robin said, "Maybe we could take the boat out now. If that's ok with you, Melanie…and you Greg."

"We were hoping you would say that," Greg said.

The smile he beamed at Robin told me Dr. P had every reason to worry. I don't know what Robin felt about Greg, but if that smile had arms they would be encircling Robin like an octopus. Her attention was completely on Melanie, however. I had no sense at all of any attraction to Greg.

She wrenched her gaze from Melanie and turned to me and Tim. "That's if we have time to x-ray the hawks first, before you have to go, Greg."

"We can do it right away," Tim said. "It won't take long. Maybe you could just help with Caboose."

"Hawks?" Greg asked.

"I volunteer here," Robin said, "They are teaching me to work with wounded raptors."

"That's your job?" Melanie asked, wide-eyed. "You work with hurt birds?"

Robin paused. I suspected I knew why she had not divulged her identity to Melanie. What little girl would be excited to discover her mom was a prostitute?

"That's my work *now*," Robin said finally.

Dr. Pritchett looked at her with such love and compassion that I knew she had talked with him at least about her profession, if not her progeny.

"Well then," Tim said, "Melanie and all the rest of you can watch, but you'll need to stand back so no one scares the hawks before we have them subdued."

"How did you get to do such a wonderful job?!" Melanie asked Robin.

Robin shifted her eyes at me. I could almost see the lifetime of shame and guilt choking her. With a deep sigh, she managed a weak grin at the child and said, "I think God decided someone named for a bird should know how to help other hurt birds."

16

After the boat ride, and after Greg and Melanie had left to return home with the boat in tow, Robin told us the whole story. There was still one last little surprise that I had not yet deduced, though I should have figured it out. Really, the clues were all there.

"All right," Mom said as soon as the door shut on Greg and Melanie, "Spill. Who is Greg to you and why didn't you tell us you had a daughter?"

"And why doesn't Melanie know you are her mother?" I asked.

"She does now," Robin said.

"You told her on your boat ride?" I asked.

"Yes. It felt like it was time."

Mom herded us into the trailer and pulled out a kitchen chair for me as she and Robin sank onto the couch.

"The whole story," Mom said.

Robin sighed. "I'm sorry I didn't tell you everything, but I did tell you most things."

"Except your real name, or that you had a child with Greg..." Mom said.

"Greg is not the father," Robin said. "And I was afraid. Not for me. I would have gone right to the police if it was just me who was in danger."

"For who then? Who was in danger?" Mom asked. I could tell she was a little peeved. She had been friends with Robin for two months, letting her share her home. I guess I couldn't blame her for being miffed.

"Melanie," Robin said.

We both sagged in our chairs. Melanie?

"When I was still in Miami, still under the thumb of Connor, I got pregnant. That's what made me run. I knew if he found out I was pregnant, he'd force me to abort...just like he had the last baby. I couldn't do that again. I just couldn't. And so I ran, and started my new life in the Gulf area...That's when I met Greg. I knew I couldn't abort, but I also knew I was unfit to be a mother. How could I ever tell my child she was the product of a corrupt cop and a hooker? Greg had just lost his wife to cancer. They'd always wanted kids…never could have them. What a laugh that is, huh? Here I'd had three abortions just throwing away in the garbage what Greg would have given anything to have.

"Anyway, he knew everything about me, including the fact of Melanie. He offered to adopt her when she was born. He told me if at any time I wanted to share my life with her, he would be willing to let me. When I ran from Connor this time, I knew if he ever knew about Melanie, he would use her to try and threaten me. Greg called me while I was here. You knew that. It was not just about the boat. Connor had contacted Melanie's teacher. Was asking about her parents. Greg felt certain he had somehow figured out she was my daughter. I don't know if he had seen her, and knew she was mine since she looks just like me or how he found her. But he didn't know he was the father. At least I don't think so. I assume he figured Greg was. If he knew Melanie was his kid, not only was I afraid he'd threaten to harm her, but if he managed to throw me in jail, he'd have legal rights to her. I couldn't let that happen. I was trapped."

Mom patted Robin's hand shaking her head.

"That creep," she said.

Robin nodded.

"So when Greg found out that Connor had been caught, and is looking at a murder and attempted murder charge and about a zillion years in jail, he knew it was time for Melanie to meet me. She knew she was adopted, but never knew who her mother was. But she had been asking."

"Does she know…" Mom paused here.

"No," Robin said, "I think she is too young to know about my…past…or about her father. Maybe when she is much older. Greg thinks we should consult with some shrinks about that, to know how much or when to share."

"How did she respond when you told her you were her mom?" I asked.

Robin chuckled. "She said she was glad because I was the prettiest lady she'd ever seen."

"She's right about that," Mom said.

"Wait till she finds out about what I am inside."

"I know how you feel," Mom said. "When Leah's father died and I finally crawled out of my drunken hole of a life, I felt nothing but shame. It was touch and go for a while whether I would kill myself or not. I had to come face to face with the ugliness of what I was, but even worse, what I had done to Leah."

She shot a quick look at me. I met her eyes and gave her a little smile. We didn't talk about all that muck very often. Too painful for both of us, but the past two years of wading my way through the Bible and Hank's counsel had somehow erased the razor sharp stab of painful memory.

"How did you forgive yourself?" Robin asked.

"When I became a Christian, I knew God forgave me. Jesus went to a lot of trouble and pain to pave that road for me. It was a whole different thing to forgive myself. I beat myself up over who I'd been for a long time. It was a long process, but in the end, I guess I decided I was telling God His path of forgiveness was not enough if Jesus could forgive me, but I couldn't. Someone else, maybe even it was Pastor Rimerton, told me that guilt is God's way of getting us to change behavior, but shame is Satan's way of holding us in bondage. If we know Christ, there is no more place for shame. We are His children, and He loves us."

"Melanie asked me why I didn't love her enough to keep her."

"What did you tell her?" Mom asked.

"I couldn't answer. I didn't know what to say. How could I tell her I didn't want her to be raised by a prostitute or a dirty cop? All that mess in her genetic makeup! How could I tell her that? Greg stepped in. He told her that when he met me, I was in a very bad situation that no child should have to endure. He told her I placed her for adoption because I loved her too much to keep her."

"That was a good answer," I said.

"But when she finds out the whole truth," Robin said, "One day she is sure to ask. How will she ever forgive me?"

"Maybe that's a question for Leah," Mom said.

I guess Mom knew how much I had struggled with forgiveness. I felt a little bad for how long it had taken me to lessen the grip of bitterness she caused in my spirit. If I could have released it sooner, I would have. At least knowing what I knew now. The anger and pain of holding on to my hatred of what she'd done to me was a heavy burden. It was a relief to let it go. But maybe until I did it, there was no way to know how much better I would feel. It was a process for me, and I am not sure I could have made it go any quicker.

Robin filled the silence with another question, "And now all the stigma of being adopted. Not even knowing her father, and I hope she never does!"

"We are all adopted," Mom said.

We are? That was news to me. "Something you want to tell me, Mom?"

"It was the sermon a few weeks ago. About the part in Romans where we are described as heirs of Christ. Let me read it to you. Just a sec."

She went back to the bedroom for her Bible. This alone was inconceivable just two years ago. Not only that my mother would leave her alcohol addiction behind, but would embrace God, and was now quoting scripture.

She sat down, and flipped through the Bible till she found the book of Romans. "Listen, this is in Romans, chapter 8: *For you did not receive the spirit of slavery to fall back into fear, but you have received the Spirit of adoption as sons, by whom we cry, "Abba! Father!" The Spirit himself bears witness with our spirit that we are children of God, and if children, then heirs—heirs of God and fellow heirs with Christ, provided we suffer with him in order that we may also be glorified with him.*

"See, what Pastor Rimerton said is all of us are severed from any relationship with God by our sin. But when we believe Jesus is Lord and raised from the dead and ask Him into our lives, we are immediately adopted by God. We become His children, and will inherit His kingdom. There is no shame in adoption, Robin."

"That part about slavery to fear. That sounds like a slogan for my life," Robin said.

"Mine too," Mom agreed. "Fear of living a single day without some sort of numbing drug. My childhood was pretty much a steady state of horror, just like yours. That doesn't exactly create well-adjusted children. I didn't know how to let go of all that fear. And then I didn't claim to believe in God, but I did know if there was a Hell, that's where I was headed. I joked about it, but in reality, it scared me to death."

Robin nodded like she was completely relating to mom's creeped out childhood.

"I used to say I couldn't wait to go to Hell since that was where all the fun-loving people went," Robin said.

"Yeah, fun loving folks like Hitler and Connor," Mom said. "If walking away from God was so much fun, why was I stuck in a bottle of booze every night? Why was my husband shooting up till his arms were like a pin cushion and his heart finally was too full of drugs to function?"

This was a super endearing little bonding time, but if you want to know the truth, I was stuck on that last line Mom had read. We are heirs with Christ, *provided* we suffer with Him.

That was the catch to the whole adoption bounty. We got to inherit whatever God our father had in store for us…but first we would suffer. I don't know about you, but that gave me pause. I was surprised when Robin brought that very point up next.

"What does that part mean about suffering with Him in order to be glorified with Him?" she asked.

"That part is not as easy to explain," Mom said.

Hank and I had had many conversations about the role of suffering on the path to God. Maybe it was the Holy Spirit, or maybe it was that I had learned a thing or two about suffering on my own path, but I had a thought, which I blurted out now.

"If life were too pleasant, what would make us long for God?"

Both Mom and Robin turned to stare at me.

"Go on," Robin said.

"Well, if we worship creation over God, Hank told me that is idolatry. And one of the Ten Commandments says we shall have no other Gods than God Himself. So that verse Mom quoted talked about being glorified with Christ. That means we are to be like Him in a way we are not right now. And Hank told me that being with God and becoming more like Him every day is the goal. But if we never suffered here on earth, why would we look to God for our joy? We wouldn't need Him if we were satisfied by what He created for us instead of Him Himself. We would turn creation into our idol, instead of the Creator Himself."

"I'm not sure I get your point," Robin said. "How does suffering make us want to be with God more? In my life, it made me hate Him."

"I guess it depends on how you suffer. If in your suffering you just rely on yourself to get out of whatever is causing the suffering or grow bitter, then it makes you run from God. But if you suffer and rely on God to end it, or to get through it, you change. You learn to rely on Him, and long for Him instead of trusting that all the things of earth will be your salvation. They never are anyway. I found that out by the time I was sixteen."

"Yes," Robin agreed, "So did I. But I didn't look to God for help. He was never around when I called."

"That's what I thought too," Mom said, "And a bottle of whiskey always was. But eventually, the whiskey almost destroyed me. I had nothing to lose in trying to see what happened if instead I trusted God to be there even when I couldn't see Him."

"And was He?" Robin asked.

"He brought me to soberness…and back to Leah."

"How do you know it was God and not just your own willpower?" Robin asked.

"I tried willpower for forty years," Mom said.

"Hank told me God is the will to my won't," I said.

"That's good," Mom said laughing. "God helped me do what I could not do. Not only stop drinking but I couldn't save myself from any sin. If I could, Jesus could have taken a nice vacation to the Bahamas instead of dying on the cross for me."

"I wish there was another way other than suffering," Robin said.

"I bet Jesus did too," I said.

"Pastor Rimerton said that suffering brings perseverance. That's a verse in Romans too. Pastor said that suffering kicks any notion of self-reliance right out of our brains when we figure out that there is nothing on earth, no person or thing, that can relieve our suffering. That's when we learn to rely on God…if we persevere. And if we persevere enough, our faith and trust in the only one who can relieve all suffering in the end grows."

"But I did rely on God…at first," Robin said. "I was just a kid. I prayed, I BEGGED God to help me. Day after day I was tortured, and finally gave up praying."

I could not resolve the tension Robin's experience created in me. I wish I could have. This is why God should never trust me to be the one expected to help with questions of faith. It is not that her question changed my belief that God was in control and that He had been in some way working on her behalf. But I could not come up with a good reason why God would allow a child to suffer in a world beyond her control.

That sparked a thought.

"You did learn something important," I said.

'Besides that my father was a devil?"

"Yes. I only say this because I learned the same thing…and in the end, it led me to God. The world was beyond your control. It was beyond mine. It is beyond anyone's control. That is why we need God. I don't know why He made you suffer so much…or at least allowed it. He could have stopped it and He didn't. I get your anger. I had it too. I guess I still do at times. But in a way, it helps me to know there are things outside my control, but never outside God's. I may suffer but He does promise there will be a time…an eternity…when I won't. I would rather trust *that* than all the things on earth that will definitely pass away and can't end my suffering anyway."

"Wow," Mom said, "Hank is wearing off on you."

Robin took a deep breath and stood up. "It's time to feed the birds," she said. "Thanks, both of you, for all this. Whatever was so frozen inside of me really feels like it is beginning to thaw. Maybe that's God. Maybe it's just talking about it. Maybe it was meeting Melanie and she seems so happy, so normal. I never talked this way with anyone before. I never really had friends before. I never even thought I needed or wanted them."

Maybe God was answering her prayers…but they'd been unvoiced. I kept that to myself because I knew what hell her life had been and perhaps it would be small comfort. However, for some reason, the thought comforted *me*.

17

I may have been a vision of loveliness, but I was quaking in my new white shoes. The swamp yard had been transformed with white ribbons and pots of flowers lining a path to a makeshift altar where Pastor Rimerton stood. Mom waited at my side, ready to walk me down the aisle. I glanced around the corner of the house to see our few guests all quiet in expectation. As I'd requested, Zippy had on a white kerchief with a ring box tied to her collar. She was the ring bearer. William Spear held her leash and Mandy Rimerton, the little girl Zippy had rescued from a child abductor two years ago sat beside him with her mom on the other side of her. Mandy would walk my ring-bearing dog to us when it was time for the ring ceremony. William would guide little Mandy on when to start down the aisle. He sat next to Miss Beam, who was doing what she does best…beaming.

On the other side of the aisle stood Lightning, behind the back row of folding chairs. Sue Middleton held her halter lead. I noticed white silk flowers had been woven in her mane. That was a nice touch. I wondered who had been responsible for that.

The small group of the rest of my friends had hushed and were looking back to the house now. I glanced back at the river, wondering if Flash and his family would show up. They had such an uncanny habit of appearing just at the right time that I fully expected them. However, if they were around at all, they were submerged.

Robin smoothed her pale pink dress in place. Her hair shimmered in the sunlight. She had died it back to her original blond. She stood beside me, waiting for the music which was her cue to start down the path. On her arm dangled a basket filled with rose petals.

I know what you are thinking. Flower girls are supposed to be innocent little girls, and Robin was about the furthest thing possible from an innocent little girl. Just hold your horses. I won't spoil the surprise.

Fortunately, we discovered that Janice Mickleburr, my old college composition teacher, was a guitar player. She offered to play the processional music which was by a group called Band of Horses. I had never heard the song before, *The Marry Song,* and neither had

Hank but we both agreed it was appropriate. Miss Mickleburr said she would play a more traditional song but she didn't feel I was a traditional bride and perhaps this one would suit me better.

If you have never heard the song before, it is worth listening to. It had some of my favorite themes of the past two years of my life since meeting Hank, including forgiveness, eternity, and lightening each other's load in life. While God is not specifically mentioned, Hank and I agreed that it reminded us of God. God had certainly lightened our load.

There is one symbolic phrase in there that Miss Mickleburr said was a perfect symbol for what a husband and wife should be to each other. She played the song for both Hank and me while we were trying to decide the song to which I should walk down the aisle. The groom is singing to his bride and reminds her of how he "keeled the wheelbarrow" he borrowed. She smiled at me when my eyes lit up and tears began to stream like a geyser.

"I get it!" I cried.

"I knew you would," she said smiling, still strumming the haunting tune on her guitar.

"Then help me out," Hank said.

"A wheelbarrow is all tottery. If you try to carry a heavy load, it is really easy to topple." I knew that because I cleaned Lightning's shed and loaded the manure sky high and then tried to maneuver over the rutted driveway to the reeds on the far side of the field where I dumped the load. Almost always, if I overloaded the wheelbarrow, it fell over with the first bump letting all that stinky mess sail all around me.

"That's true," Hank agreed. "I can see where a wheelbarrow full to the brim could be a symbol of the rocky road of marriage. A lot of people struggle in relationships...but is that really what we want to be our song to memorialize the beginning of our life together?"

"But he keels the wheelbarrow. The keel is what weighs the boat down in the water so that it doesn't fall over with every passing wave. God is our keel."

Hank's smile widened, and he hugged me. "Very good!"

"You see why she was my star pupil," Miss Mickleburr said. "But why is it borrowed?"

I settled back to think over that one.

"The load will not always be there," Hank said, "There will come a day when there will be no need of the wheelbarrow at all."

I nodded. "I see. *Come all ye who are heavy-laden and I will give you rest for your souls.*"

"I'm impressed!" Hank said.

"Don't be," I said, "Mom quoted that verse to Robin during one of our discussions while feeding the hawks."

"I like the song then very much," Hank said. "You sing it beautifully, Janice."

"I like it too," I said. "Maybe my mom should push me down the aisle in a wheelbarrow?"

Hank thought I was kidding. I was…but not about Lightning's role in the wedding which he thought was just me kidding as well.

As the guitar chords rose above the sound of the river, Robin started down the aisle. When she reached Lightning, she took the lead rope and leading my dear horse, began tossing rose petals along the path. It would have been even more beautiful if Lightning didn't stop every few feet to gobble up the rose petals, but it still was an awesome moment for me. Lightning had paved my path when I first arrived to this place as a terrified homeless teen. Now she was sweetening the path to my husband, although in truth she was chowing down as much of the sweetness as she could get away with.

Robin was not much of a horse person and didn't dare jerk too hard on the lead to dissuade Lightning from her feast of roses. It would have all ended in the whole crowd deciding our wedding was a comedy act except for the moving message of Miss Mickleburr's song.

Mom and I followed when Lightning was halfway to Hank. I was glad I let Hank talk me into a real wedding dress. I did feel like a princess and was surprised how it was nice to feel like the star of a fairy tale. My life had not been even close to a fairy tale for the first sixteen years. The last three though…. what a ride!

Lightning and Robin stood on the side of the aisle opposite Hank. Hank stood with Dr. Pritchett watching me with a steady gaze. Hank always made me feel like I was the most important person on earth, but now he made me feel like I was the ONLY one on earth. If you have never felt that way, maybe you married the wrong person.

Dr. P on the other hand was watching Robin. I suspected there would be another wedding in our happy swamp soon.

As the song ended with that fantastic verse about keeling the borrowed wheelbarrow, I stood adjacent to Hank. Out of the corner of my eye, I saw Lightning eating the remaining rose petals in the basket.

Robin shrugged at me, clearly having no idea how to prevent her from doing so.

"Who gives this woman in marriage?" Pastor Rimerton asked.

Now, you might not believe this, and I almost didn't believe it myself, but right on that cue, not only did Mom say, "I do", but there was an explosion of splashing behind us in the river. We all swung around in time to see Flash and Pinky leaping into the air, and falling back to the river. I told you they had uncanny timing. I am not making this up.

Pastor Rimerton waited for the laughter to die down, and then told mom she could sit down. She kissed my cheek and whispered, 'I love you." I was surprised to hear myself echo that back. Hank moved to my side and took my hand. He squeezed his palm against mine.

"Well, we are finally here," Pastor Rimerton said to Hank and me. "A wedding where two people are joined together before God is always a special ceremony to preside over, but this one gives me special pleasure. I have you to thank for the safe return of my child, and you both are especially precious in our family's heart. But also, for two years I have watched the miracle of God transforming lives in a most unlikely way from so much bondage and adversity to freedom and joy in knowing Him. Your life Leah, and that of your mother and so many of the people whose lives you have touched" (here he looked over at Robin) "have been a testament to the power of Christ in the midst of terrible struggle to redeem and reclaim.

"Hank has long been a young man after God's heart, and it is fitting that he has found a young woman to share his passion and delight in serving others as the hands and feet of Christ on earth. We stand here in the shadow of an aviary designed to heal wounded birds. It is a fitting place for a wedding. No matter how perfect each of you see the other to be today in all your beautiful wedding clothes with your future stretching out filled with possibilities before you, there will be times in your life together when you will be wounded, and even sometimes feel it is more than you can bear.

"Christ Himself warns us that in this world you will have troubles, but take heart, *for I have overcome the world.* He does not promise that your lives will be trouble free, but He does promise that He will be with you through those trials. His example of sacrificial love to His people is often depicted as the way a groom should love his bride. We are cherished by God in the same way as Hank cherishes you today, Leah. Just as Christ is willing to lay down His life for God's people, Hank is charged to protect and provide for you sacrificially.

"The forgiveness Christ extends to each of us we are to in turn extend to others. There is a terrible line from an old movie, 'Love means never having to say you're sorry.' That does a great disservice to true love. Love means *always* having to say you're sorry. Those three words are almost as important as *I Love You.*

"One of the sad hallmarks of humanity is that we will fail each other. We will hurt each other. We will disappoint, annoy, and sometimes even damage each other. I know this is perhaps not what you want to hear at this point in your new life together, Leah and Hank, but it is sandwiched with an important critical message of Hope. When we express sorrow over our failings to each other, we open the door to forgiveness and healing.

"In the Lord's Prayer, we are advised to forgive as we are forgiven. We are to forgive without limit. We are also told that while we were yet sinners, Christ forgave us. Before we ever said we were sorry, we were forgiven.

"But dear ones, forgiveness is not the same as reconciliation. Christ forgives us, but to be fully reconciled to God in a right relationship with God, we must repent, tell Him we are sorry for our sins against Him. The Bible speaks of a 'Godly sorrow' that leads to repentance. Without sorrow or recognition or acceptance of when we have failed each other, relationships flounder, and even die. If we are to forgive as Christ forgave us and have full restoration of the relationship God desires with us and for us, we must know that love must say *I am sorry* when we have wronged each other.

"Leah and Hank, at this moment perhaps you cannot envision any time when your precious spouse will disappoint you. As a married man of ten years now, I am sure my wife will attest to the truth—just wait. He will. She will.

"There is nothing as wonderful as a good marriage on earth…but that relationship does not supplant your relationship with God. Your spouse is not God, and therefore not perfect. He will fail. She will fail. But God has joined you in Holy Matrimony, and what God has joined together, none should put asunder.

"If you remember to keep God first and expect perfection only from God alone, and be willing to forgive your spouse when necessary, and to apologize when you have wronged the other, the blessings and strength of Christ will fill your hearts and your home."

I noticed a fluttering at my side. It was Robin wiping wet cheeks. A thin line of mascara marred her perfect complexion.

"And now, we ask the ring bearer to approach the altar."

At this, William gave little Mandy a nod and she took Zippy's leash from his hand. It all started well, exactly as we had practiced, but then little Mandy wasn't prepared for Zippy's lunge forward to come say hello to me and Hank. He yanked the leash from her hand and the race was on. I won't go through all the gory details here, but if you are planning to run a marathon, I don't recommend you do it in a wedding dress.

We finally managed to step on the leash bringing Zippy to a yipping halt. I was relieved to see the ring box still securely tied to his collar, both rings intact.

Zippy licked Hank's hand as he detached the box from the collar. Mandy had made her way to the front of the aisle now, with her mother in tow, and the two clutched Zippy's leash and moved to the side beside the weeping and chuckling Robin, and Lightning who was still nibbling rose petals.

"These rings are a symbol not only of your devotion and pledge one to another, but also of the eternal encircling of God's arms around you both and around your marriage. As the ring has no beginning and no end, may it remind you of the infinite, eternal love of God for you, and for each other.

"Now Leah, Hank, please turn and face each other. Do you, Hank, take this woman Leah to be your lawfully wedded wife, to have and to cherish, to honor and to love, through better or for worse, for so long as you both shall live?"

"I do," Hank said. Zippy barked, and lunged again, but Mrs. Rimerton was helping Mandy hang on. Hank smiled, looking deeply into my eyes as he slipped the ring on my finger.

"Leah, do you take this man Hank, to be your lawfully wedded husband, to love and respect and be a help-mate to him through sickness and in health, through good times and bad till death do you part?"

"I do," I whispered.

I waited expecting dolphins to crash in the background, but their benediction was done for the day. Lightning nickered, but I doubt it was in support of me so much as complaining that the rose petals were gone.

"By the power vested in me by the Holy Father above, I now pronounce you husband and wife. You may kiss the bride."

Our first married kiss! You don't need to hear how bells and whistles started clanging or how my knees turned into rubber. I'm sure you have heard all the platitudes.

It was the first wedding I had ever attended, but if you ask me, it was the best wedding any wedding could be! A new beginning, a magical ending to my unlikely story…but really, how else could it have ended?

The End

Author's Note

As in all my stories, this series began from issues I was struggling with in my walk with God. None of it is biographical except in the sense that all my work relates to who I am and what I am learning as I journey through life.

I am deeply grateful to Amy Fox, my editor, who dropped everything in her busy life to help me in the edit and final ideas for this book. My wonderful niece, Sergeant Renee Carlson of Pima County Sheriff Department, gave me wonderful feedback on police related issues. Any mistakes or inaccuracies are my fault, not hers.

I am thankful for my parents who read the rough draft and provided their insights in how I could improve the story.

Most of all, I am indebted to God who sends me daily inspiration in the beauty and grandeur of His creation and His Word. I still cannot believe that the creator of the universe wants anything to do with me…but it is clear, He does.

John 15:15

I no longer call you servants, because a servant does not know his master's business. Instead, I have called you friends, for everything that I learned from my Father I have made known to you.

Other Books by Vicky Kaseorg

Listening with a Broken Ear- 2011
God Drives a Tow Truck- 2011
Tommy- a Story of Ability- 2012
Turning Points-The Life of a Milne Bay WWII Gunner- 2012
The Illustrated 23rd Psalm- 2012
The Good Parent- 2012
The Well-Trained Human- 2012
Saving a Dog- 2014
The Tower Builder – 2014
The Bark of the Covenant – 2014
Poppy- The Dirty Ditch Digging Dingo – 2015
The Paws That Bring Good News – 2015
Joe- The Horse Nobody Loved – 2015
Gidget- The Horse Formerly Known as Witch- 2015
Gidget- The Horse I Didn't Own- 2015
Gidget- The Horse That Waited For Me- 2015
Singing in the Darkness – 2016
Perhaps You Misheard My Prayer – 2016
Unlikely Friends – 2016
Unlikely Redemption – 2016
Unlikely Rescue - 2017

To Connect with Vicky Kaseorg

I love to hear from readers! Your comments and feedback are a continual inspiration. Please sign up for email updates to my publications at my Facebook author or blog page.

Visit my Facebook page and "like" it for regular updates on new books/writing. I love to hear from readers!

www.facebook.com/pages/Vicky-aseorgAuthor/344952178879131

Twitter: https://twitter.com/vickykaseorg

Follow me on my daily inspirational blog at vickykaseorg.blogspot.com

Stay abreast of new publications at my author page at: http://www.amazon.com/Vicky-Kaseorg/e/B006XJ2DWU

If you enjoyed this book, please go to Amazon, or wherever you purchased this book, and write a review! Much appreciated!

Amazon site: http://www.amazon.com/gp/product/B015ANTRMS?*Version*=1&*entries*=0

Also, reviews are critical to all authors. Please visit the site where you purchased this book. I would be very grateful for your review.

Sign up for mailing list of new releases and specials at: http://eepurl.com/bp-EEP

Unlikely Reward

Unlikely Reward

www.ingramcontent.com/pod-product-compliance
Lightning Source LLC
Chambersburg PA
CBHW050916260726
48660CB00001B/231